THE 7 LOVE LANGUAGES OF BLACK MEN

MICHAEL DARBY

Copyright © 2025 by Michael Darby

All rights reserved.

ISBN paperback: 979-8-218-74210-2

No portion of this book may be reproduced in any form without written permission from the publisher or author, except as permitted by U.S. copyright law.

This publication is designed to provide accurate and authoritative information in regard to the subject matter covered. It is sold with the understanding that neither the author nor the publisher is engaged in rendering legal, investment, accounting or other professional services. While the publisher and author have used their best efforts in preparing this book, they make no representations or warranties with respect to the accuracy or completeness of the contents of this book and specifically disclaim any implied warranties of merchantability or fitness for a particular purpose. No warranty may be created or extended by sales representatives or written sales materials. The advice and strategies contained herein may not be suitable for your situation. You should consult with a professional when appropriate. Neither the publisher nor the author shall be liable for any loss of profit or any other commercial damages, including but not limited to special, incidental, consequential, personal, or other damages.

1st edition 2025

THE 7 LOVE LANGUAGES OF BLACK MEN

**How to Build Stronger Relationships and Heal from Trauma
A New Framework for Healing, Connection, and Authentic Love**

How to use this Book

This book is designed to serve multiple audiences, each with unique needs and perspectives. Here's how to engage with this content for maximum impact:

For Black Men

Read each chapter personally first, then share key insights with your partner. Use the growth practices consistently—transformation happens through repetition, not just revelation. Don't try to master all seven love languages at once. Focus on understanding your primary love language first, then gradually expand your emotional vocabulary. Remember: this journey is about becoming more fully yourself, not becoming someone else.

For Partners of Black Men

Focus first on understanding before seeking to be understood. Each love language represents decades of learned survival—honor the strength while supporting the growth. Your patience during this process isn't just kindness; it's participation in generational healing. When he expresses love in his primary language, receive it as the gift it is, even as you help him expand his expression.

For Therapists and Counselors

This framework can revolutionize your work with Black male clients. Use the "raw and refined" concept to meet clients where they are while supporting their evolution. These love languages are often trauma responses that became survival strategies. Honor them first, then help refine them. Cultural competence isn't optional—it's essential for effective treatment.

For Pastors and Community Leaders

These love languages are pathways to emotional liberation that honor both cultural strength and biblical wholeness. Use this framework in men's ministry, marriage counseling, and community healing initiatives. Remember: emotional intelligence isn't optional for spiritual leadership—it's essential for shepherding God's people effectively.

Contents

Dedication	VI
Acknowledgements	VII
Preface: The Language of Healing	VIII
Intoduction: Why Black Men Need Their own Love Languages	X
Chapter 1: Presence as Protection	1
Chapter 2: Provision as Expression	9
Chapter 3: Respect as Intimacy	17
Chapter 4: Loyalty as Language	25
Chapter 5: Sacrifice as Devotion	33
Chapter 6: Affirmation as Healing	39
Chapter 7: Touch as Trust	47
Chapter 8: Love Language Fluency	57
Chapter 9: Into Me See - A Black Man's Declaration	69
Appendix A: Love Language Assessment and Growth Practices	83
Appendix B: Resources for Continued Healing	89
Appendix C: Quick Reference Guide	95
About the author	103

To my father, who loved us with tools he had to forge himself.
It took me years to understand the depth of his devotion,
to see past my own expectations of the man
who carried burdens I never knew existed.

His father had even fewer resources,
and the crushing weight of Jim Crow left scars that shaped generations.
Yet in silence, my father absorbed the blows of my ignorance—
the criticism for not being the father I thought I needed,
when he was exactly the father he knew how to be.
My healing has allowed me to see him more clearly now.
I am better because of his sacrifices, stronger because of his quiet endurance.

To my children—Averi, Cameron, and Israel—
who have shown me grace beyond measure.
They have watched me stumble and grow as a father, offering understanding
when I deserved judgment, love when I felt unworthy.
I am nothing without their love, and I will spend my life continuing to earn the
right to be their father.

And to all the men who continue to press toward the mark—
who choose growth over comfort, healing over hurt, love over legacy wounds—
this is for you.

Acknowledgements

To my parents, who have 54 years in this thing called love—because I have had the honor to watch and observe them, I still hold hope that love like theirs exists for a man like me. To my children, Always & Forever.

I want to thank Heidi, my first therapist. I ran this white woman through it. It took some years to open, but she helped me understand how trust should work. I'm glad I learned to trust you. To Quinita, my first Black therapist—I'm not here without you. It's just that simple.

I want to thank all the Black men who have knowingly and often unknowingly provided me with the experiences and scenarios that helped shape these 7 Love Languages. To all the barbershops that provided the perfect environment to hear our voices free from cancel culture and unjust scrutiny: Champions Portland, Hemisphere (Seattle—my guy Eric Clark), Major League crew (Sean, Kel, Adrian, Dom, Coup), The Influential.

I want to acknowledge Fear. I see why you're necessary. For many years you kept me paralyzed, and I sat on this book. Now when I sense you, I understand it's a sign I'm headed in the right direction.

Lastly, God, I thank you for every gift you've given, and I'm just now beginning to see I don't have to be boxed into any one or two things. I can walk in the authority you gave Adam and seize the land, letting my gifts make room.

Preface: The Language of Healing

Every language begins with the need to be understood.

For too long, Black men have been speaking love languages that the world refused to recognize, expressing care in dialects shaped by survival, offering affection through actions forged in environments where vulnerability meant danger and emotional expression could be fatal.

We've been told we don't know how to love when the truth is we've been loving in languages the world wouldn't learn to speak. Critics condemned our emotional expression, when they should have celebrated our emotional survival.

The Bible says a good man leaves an inheritance for his children's children. But the weight the world has placed on us to be exceptional, to exceed and leap over all these chivalrous ideas about masculinity and how we show up didn't come from us. Others decided this for us without our input because, since slavery, silence and compliance were the only ways we could survive. Anything else meant death.

Like a plant stuck in a small pot or a fish left in a small bowl, neither will reach its capacity, nor even know it can produce more fruit and grow into a great white shark. We have for decades made ourselves small and compliant with no voice.

That time is over.

The 7 Love Languages of Black Men is a piece of a larger, beautiful mosaic of what good Black men are becoming—stronger and better at saying who we are, what we are not, and how God made us. If you love us, learn us through our lived experience, because that's what true love does.

I am not a therapist or counselor. I am a Black man, a father, a brother who has done the work—the hard, necessary work of healing, growth, and emotional development that I'm asking you to consider in these pages. My authority to write this book doesn't come from professional credentials. It comes from the scars I've turned to wisdom, the pain I've transformed to purpose, and the courage to be vulnerable that I'm asking of every man who reads this.

This book is different. It does not assume that Black men are emotionally broken and need fixing. It starts from the recognition that Black men have been emotionally creative and need to be understood. It honors the love languages we already speak while creating pathways for the love languages we're still learning.

The seven love languages explored in these pages aren't invented—they're discovered. They're not prescribed—they're recognized. They emerge from hundreds of conversations with Black men who've been willing to share their hearts, their struggles, and their growth. They're supported by research I've studied, refined through insights from therapy I've experienced, and tested in the crucible of real relationships I've lived.

But this is more than a book about love languages. This is a manifesto for Black male emotional liberation written by one of us, for all of us. This is a roadmap for healing that honors where we've been while pointing toward where we can go. This is an invitation to rewrite the narrative about Black men and love—not by changing who we are, but by expanding how we express who we've always been.

We have the right to define what love looks, sounds, and feels like for us. We have the right to our own emotional languages, our own healing journey, our own definition of strength that includes vulnerability, tenderness, and authentic connection. We have the right to break out of the small pots and bowls that have contained us and grow into the fullness of who God created us to be.

The language of healing begins with the courage to speak our truth, to refuse to be small anymore, to claim our voice in defining our own love. Let's find our voices together.

Intoduction: Why Black Men Need Their own Love Languages

The statistics tell a story that should break our hearts and fuel our action. Black men have the highest suicide rate increase of any demographic in America, rising 60% between 1999 and 2019. We're twice as likely to experience depression but half as likely to seek treatment. Research indicates that 56-74% of Black males exposed to traumatic events may have unmet mental health service needs, with Black male trauma survivors being significantly less likely to utilize mental health services than other demographic groups. Stress-related illness and violence cause much of the six-year difference in life expectancy between us and white men.

But behind these numbers is a deeper truth: Black men are dying emotionally long before we die physically. We suffocate in silence, drown in expectations we never chose, and carry trauma we were never taught to heal. Society has conditioned us to be strong without support, to provide without being provided for, and to protect without protection.

The traditional frameworks for understanding love and relationships—while valuable—often miss the mark in Black men's emotional reality. They don't account for the historical trauma that shapes our attachment styles, the systemic barriers that affect our ability to provide, or the cultural context that influences how we express care and receive affection. Recent research shows that adherence to traditional masculine norms negatively impacts attitudes toward seeking mental health services among African American men, creating additional barriers to emotional healing and relationship growth.

The Historical Context We Can't Ignore

To understand how Black men love, we must first understand what has shaped our capacity to love. Survival, shaped by centuries of systematic attempts to break our families, criminalize our presence, and reduce our humanity to economic productivity, forged our emotional expression.

From slavery through Jim Crow to mass incarceration, Black families have faced deliberate policies designed to separate fathers from children, husbands from wives, and men from their communities. The 1960s welfare policies included "man in the house" rules that literally made male presence an economic liability for Black families. A welfare worker could terminate benefits if they found evidence of a father living in the home. Think about what this taught generations of Black families: male presence equals economic loss, male absence equals financial survival.

The mass incarceration system removed millions of Black men from their families during their prime years, then released them with criminal records that made legitimate employment nearly impossible. This created a generation of men who couldn't provide financially even when they wanted to, while simultaneously being judged by society—and sometimes by their partners—for not being primary financial providers.

These aren't just historical footnotes—they're the foundation upon which many Black men learned to love. We learned to love in the margins, in the spaces between presence and absence, in the tension between wanting to stay and needing to survive. We learned to express care through actions because words could be dangerous, to show love through sacrifice because vulnerability could be fatal.

The Cultural Strengths We Must Reclaim

But this same history also created profound strengths that mainstream relationship literature often overlooks. Black men developed extraordinary capacities for loyalty, protection, and presence under impossible circumstances.

We learned to love through action when words were unsafe, to provide in ways that went far beyond financial support, to create safety for our families even when we couldn't find safety for ourselves.

Traditional African concepts of manhood were holistic—encompassing spiritual leadership, community building, knowledge transfer, and comprehensive care. Colonial systems deliberately dismantled these models, replacing them with industrial frameworks that reduced men to economic units. But the DNA of that holistic masculinity still lives in us, waiting to be reclaimed and refined.

The Seven Love Languages for Black Men

Through years of research, therapy, and conversations with hundreds of Black men, I've identified seven love languages that reflect our unique emotional landscape:

1. Presence as Protection: Love expressed through showing up, staying present, and creating safety through our physical and emotional availability.

2. Provision as Expression: Comprehensive care that goes beyond financial support to include emotional, spiritual, and cultural provision.

3. Respect as Intimacy: The emotional safety needed to be vulnerable, where respect creates the foundation for deeper connection.

4. Loyalty as Language: Steadfast commitment that communicates love through consistency, faithfulness, and choosing to stay even when it's difficult.

5. Sacrifice as Devotion: Giving from fullness rather than depletion, learning to serve without self-erasure.

6. Affirmation as Healing: Words that rebuild identity, restore confidence, and create emotional safety for growth.

7. Touch as Trust: Nonsexual, affirming physical connection that communicates safety, acceptance, and emotional presence.

The Raw and Refined Framework

Each love language exists on a spectrum from "raw" to "refined." The raw expression is honest and real—spoken from survival, shaped by trauma, but authentic to where we are in our healing journey. The refined expression is that same truth, but processed through healing, reflection, and a willingness to be understood.

This framework honors where Black men are while creating pathways for where we can grow. It doesn't shame the raw expression—it recognizes it as a starting point for transformation. It doesn't demand perfection—it invites evolution.

Who This Book Is For

This book is for Black men who have been told they don't know how to love, when the truth is they've been loving in ways the world refuses to recognize. It's for men who are tired of being misunderstood, who want to expand their emotional vocabulary without abandoning their authentic selves.

It's for the women who love Black men—wives, partners, daughters, mothers, sisters—who want to understand the language we speak before we learn to speak theirs. It's for those who see our efforts but want to help us grow, who recognize our love but long for deeper connection.

It's for therapists, pastors, counselors, and healers who want to meet Black men where we are, not where they think we should be. This resource is for anyone believing healing is possible, love is learnable, and Black men deserve frameworks honoring their complexity and supporting their growth.

The Promise of This Work

This book promises something revolutionary: that good Black men who choose to do the work can learn to love more fully without losing their authentic selves. That we can become emotionally fluent without abandoning our cultural identity. That we can heal our trauma while honoring our resilience. That we can expand our love languages while maintaining our strength.

The Bible says a good man leaves an inheritance for his children's children. For too long, the inheritance we've been passing down has been survival strategies disguised as love languages—ways of caring that were shaped by systems that never asked our permission, never sought our input, never honored our voice.

Since slavery, being silent and compliant was the only way we could literally survive. Anything else meant death. So we learned to make ourselves small, to fit into the containers others made for us, to speak love in whispers when our hearts wanted to roar. Like a plant stuck in a small pot or a fish confined to a small bowl, we could never reach our capacity because we didn't even know we were capable of producing more fruit, of growing into the great white sharks we were designed to be.

I am not a therapist or counselor with degrees on the wall. I am a Black man and father who has chosen to work on himself—who has sat in therapy sessions, read extensively, engaged with research, and most importantly, listened to the stories and hearts of other Black men who are on this same journey of growth and healing.

My authority to write this book comes not from professional credentials, but from the lived experience of an everyday Black man who refused to accept that we don't know how to love. It comes from years of conversations in barbershops, therapy offices, and late-night phone calls with brothers who are choosing vulnerability over invulnerability, healing over hurt, voice over silence.

This book is for every good Black man whom others have misunderstood, whom others have told that his way of loving isn't enough, and whom others have criticized for emotional expression shaped by survival. It's written by one of you, for all of us, because we deserve to define what love looks like in our own voices and on our own terms.

The 7 Love Languages of Black Men is a piece of a larger, beautiful mosaic of what good Black men are becoming—stronger and better at saying who we are, what we are not, and how God made us. If you love us, learn us through our lived experience, because that's what true love does.

The journey toward emotional fluency isn't about becoming someone else—it's about becoming more fully ourselves. It's about breaking out of the small pots that have contained us and growing into the fullness God intended. It's about taking the love we've always carried and learning to express it in ways that create deeper connection, stronger relationships, and healthier families.

This is more than a book about love languages. This is a manifesto for Black male emotional liberation written by a Black man who has done the work and is committed to helping other Black men do the same. This is a roadmap for healing that honors where we've been while pointing toward where we can go. This is an invitation to rewrite the narrative about Black men and love—not by changing who we are, but by expanding how we express who we've always been.

That time of being small and silent is over. The language of healing begins with the courage to speak our own truth, to claim our voice in defining our own love, to leave an inheritance of emotional freedom for our children's children.

Let's find our voices together.

Chapter 1: Presence as Protection

Love Language 1
"Just because he doesn't speak doesn't mean he's absent. Some men love in silence because the world punished them for making noise." — Dr. Thema Bryant

Opening Reflection

Many Black men were not raised to say, "I love you," but we were taught—directly or indirectly—to protect.

We express care through action: working long hours, covering bills, ensuring our loved ones are safe. We sit in silence, observe what others miss, and stand close when life becomes unpredictable. For many of us, being present is how we express love when we lack the tools to articulate what we feel.

We come from environments where vulnerability could be dangerous, where silence was safety, and where presence became our clearest demonstration of love. Our presence is not passive. It is protective. It is how we signal loyalty, care, and emotional investment.

But presence without communication can be misinterpreted as disinterest. For partners seeking verbal affirmation or emotional availability, presence alone may feel hollow. This gap creates emotional distance, even when both partners are deeply invested. It is not neglect—it is a difference in emotional language.

Dr. Jor-El Caraballo, LMHC, who specializes in Black male mental health, explains the deeper psychological foundation: "Black men often have a hard time identifying their feelings and showing vulnerabilities with people in our lives. One of the best things Black men can do for their mental health is to first give themselves permission to feel." This permission to feel is revolutionary for men who learned that emotional expression could be dangerous, but it begins with understanding that our presence itself is already a form of emotional expression—one that deserves recognition and respect.

The Science Behind Protective Presence

When your nervous system learned that emotional expression was dangerous, it developed hypervigilance—constantly scanning for threats. This shows up in relationships as a man who's always alert, always watching, always ready to protect. Your presence isn't just being there; it's being there with purpose.

Recent research in trauma and attachment helps us understand why presence becomes such a primary love language for many Black men. When we've experienced chronic stress or lived in environments where we had to be constantly alert, our nervous system learns to communicate safety through physical availability rather than through words, which might feel too vulnerable or risky.

This means your presence carries emotional weight that others might not understand. When you choose to stay home instead of going out with friends, when you sit quietly while your family watches TV, when you show up to every important event—you're speaking love in a language forged by survival and refined by commitment.

Case Study: Derrick & Ciara

Derrick is a 34-year-old husband and father of two. He works six days a week, attends his children's events, and never misses a bill. In couples therapy, his wife Ciara says:

"He's always here, but I feel alone."

Derrick responds:

"I don't know what more she wants. I come home. I provide. I'm not out here in the streets. That's love to me."

Derrick's love language is Presence as Protection: he demonstrates love by showing up, staying loyal, and fulfilling responsibilities. Ciara, however, seeks emotional openness and verbal reassurance. Neither person is wrong—but they are speaking different emotional dialects.

This is not a failure of love. It is a failure of translation.

The Deeper Story Behind Derrick's Presence

During extended therapy sessions, Derrick revealed the origins of his presence-based love language. His father left when he was seven, and his mother worked two jobs to keep the family afloat. "I remember sitting by the window every Friday, waiting for him to pick me up for the weekend. Most times, he never came," Derrick shared. "I promised myself I would never do that to my kids. I would always be there."

Derrick's commitment to presence was forged in the fire of abandonment trauma. His nervous system learned that the highest form of love was simply showing up consistently. This wasn't just a preference—it was a survival strategy that became a love language.

The Transformation Process

The healing process for Derrick and Ciara took eight months of consistent therapy and intentional practice. It began with what their therapist called "love language translation"—helping each partner understand the emotional logic behind the other's primary love language.

Derrick's Growth Practices:
- **Named Presence**: Instead of just showing up, Derrick learned to name his presence. "I'm here because I choose to be here. I'm here because you matter to me."
- **Emotional Check-ins**: Twice a week, Derrick would ask Ciara, "How are you feeling about us?" and then listen without trying to fix or solve.

- **Vulnerable Presence**: Derrick began sharing one thing he was worried about or excited about each day, making his presence emotionally available, not just physically available.

Ciara's Growth Practices:

- **Presence Recognition**: Ciara began verbally acknowledging Derrick's presence. "I notice that you're here. I notice that you chose to come home to us. That means something to me."

- **Action Appreciation**: Instead of only asking for words, Ciara began appreciating the love Derrick was already expressing through his actions.

Two Years Later: Follow-Up

Derrick and Ciara now co-facilitate a couples' workshop called "Presence Plus" at their church. "Learning to translate love languages saved our marriage," Ciara reflects. "Now we help other couples understand that different doesn't mean wrong—it just means we need better translation skills."

Derrick adds: "I still show love through presence, but now I also show love through words. Ciara still needs verbal affirmation, but now she also recognizes my presence as profound love. We speak both languages fluently."

Their children have benefited most from this transformation. "Dad still doesn't talk as much as Mom," their 12-year-old son Marcus observes, "but when he sits with us during homework or comes to our games, we know he loves us. And now he tells us too."

Clinical Applications: Working with Presence-Oriented Clients

Assessment Questions:

- "Tell me about how your father (or father figures) showed love. What did that look like?"

- "When you feel most loved by someone, what are they doing? Are they saying something, or are they present in a particular way?"

- "Describe a time when someone's presence made you feel safe or cared for."

Therapeutic Interventions:

- Psychoeducation about how trauma shapes attachment and love language development

- "Presence Plus" exercises that combine physical availability with emotional engagement

- Partner education about recognizing and appreciating presence-based love expression

- Communication skills training that honors natural communication style while expanding expression

Warning Signs:

- Client becomes more withdrawn when pushed to be more verbally expressive

- Partner frustration with "silent treatment" that may actually be protective presence

- Client feels criticized for his natural way of showing love

Therapeutic Stance:

- Honor the client's presence-based love language as valid and meaningful

- Frame growth as expansion rather than replacement of existing love expression

- Help partners understand the trauma-informed nature of presence as protection

Cultural Bridge: From Ancestral Wisdom to Modern Healing

Traditional African cultures understood that male presence carried spiritual weight. The elder who sat silently during community gatherings wasn't absent—he was anchoring the space with his wisdom and watchfulness. Ubuntu philosophy—"I am because we are"—created understanding that presence itself was contribution.

Modern Black men can reclaim this by:
- Understanding that your presence has always carried emotional significance

- Creating "emotional Ubuntu"—safe spaces with other growing men where presence is honored

- Teaching partners and children to recognize presence as a profound form of love

- Expanding presence to include emotional engagement without abandoning the strength of your physical commitment

Key Takeaways from Presence as Protection:

- Your physical presence is already a love language—it just needs emotional engagement

- Trauma taught you to love through showing up; healing teaches you to show up emotionally

- "Presence Plus"—being physically AND emotionally available—transforms relationships

- Your commitment to staying is revolutionary in a world that taught Black men to leave

Next Steps:

- Practice "named presence"—tell people why you choose to be there

- Add one emotional check-in to your daily routine with your partner

- Notice when you withdraw and practice staying engaged instead

- Acknowledge when others show love through presence

Reflection Questions:

- How did you learn that presence equals love?

- What would change if you combined your physical presence with emotional availability?

- Who in your life needs to understand your presence-based love language?

- What makes it safe for you to be not just present, but emotionally present?

Chapter 2: Provision as Expression

Love Language 2

"*A man's worth is not measured by his wallet, but by his willingness to give what he has—whether that's time, attention, wisdom, or resources—from a place of love rather than obligation.*" — Dr. Michael Eric Dyson

Opening Reflection

For generations, Black men have been taught that love is spelled P-R-O-V-I-D-E. We learned that our value was measured by what we could give, our worth determined by what we could produce, our love proven by what we could sacrifice. This isn't wrong—provision is a beautiful expression of care. But when provision becomes reduced to financial performance alone, it creates a prison that exhausts the provider while limiting the depth of connection possible in relationships.

Provision as Expression is about comprehensive care that goes far beyond money. It encompasses emotional provision (creating safety and stability), spiritual provision (offering wisdom and guidance), physical provision (ensuring comfort and security), relational provision (fostering connection), and yes, material provision (meeting practical needs). When we understand provision in its fullness, we can express love through giving without losing ourselves in the process.

But to understand how Black men learned to equate love with provision, we must first understand how systematic forces deliberately reduced our understanding of manhood to economic productivity—and how this reduction was designed to break our families and communities.

The Systematic Trap: How Policy Created the Financial Prison

Before we can heal from the reduction of provision to money, we must understand how this reduction was systematically created. This wasn't organic cultural evolution—this was deliberate policy designed to separate Black families and redefine Black manhood in terms that would serve economic systems rather than strengthen communities.

The Welfare State's Assault on Black Manhood

Starting in the 1960s, welfare policies included what were called "man in the house" rules. Social workers would make unannounced visits to determine if fathers were living in the home—if evidence of a male presence was found, cases were closed and welfare checks discontinued.

Think about what this taught generations of Black families:

- Male presence = economic loss

- Male absence = financial survival

- Men = economic liability rather than holistic providers

The government literally created a system where a Black man would need to earn the equivalent of $180,000 today just to compete with government assistance. This wasn't welfare—this was economic warfare against Black male family involvement.

The Employment Marginalization

Black people are about twice as likely as white people to be unemployed, a figure that has held steady for the last seventy years. Black workers are paid less than their white counterparts at every level of employment, even with comparable qualifications.

Black men face systematic employment discrimination while simultaneously being held to the cultural standard of being primary financial providers. The system broke our economic power, then judged us for being economically broken.

Biblical Foundation: What Provision Actually Means

To reclaim a healthy understanding of provision, we must return to its original design—not as defined by capitalist systems, but as revealed in Scripture and traditional African culture.

The Genesis Model: Before Economics Existed

In Genesis 2:15, God placed Adam in the Garden "to work it and take care of it." But notice: this was before the fall, before scarcity, before economic systems. Adam's work was cultivation, stewardship, and care—not economic productivity for survival.

Biblical provision encompasses:

- **Spiritual Provision**: Leading the family in wisdom, prayer, and moral guidance

- **Emotional Provision**: Creating safety, offering comfort, providing stability

- **Physical Provision**: Protection, presence, and yes—material needs as able

- **Relational Provision**: Fostering connection between family members
- **Cultural Provision**: Passing down heritage, values, and identity

The Bible does not indicate that a good husband and father brings home all the income or even the most, but he is required to work for it to the best of his abilities. Biblical provision is comprehensive care, not just financial performance.

Case Study: Jerome's Journey from Financial Prison to Holistic Provision

Jerome, a 38-year-old father of three, came to therapy because his marriage was falling apart despite his working 70 hours a week to provide for his family. "I don't understand," he told his therapist. "I work harder than any man I know. I pay every bill. I never ask for anything for myself. But my wife says I'm not present, and my kids barely know me."

The Breaking Point

The crisis came when Jerome's 12-year-old son Marcus was caught shoplifting. When Jerome asked why, Marcus said, "I wanted to see if you would notice me if I got in trouble." Jerome realized that in his effort to provide financially, he had failed to provide emotionally, relationally, and spiritually.

The Healing Process

Jerome's healing journey involved expanding his understanding of provision from financial performance to comprehensive care:

Emotional Provision: Jerome began having weekly one-on-one time with each of his children, asking about their feelings, dreams, and challenges.

Spiritual Provision: Jerome started leading family devotions and teaching his children about their heritage, values, and faith.

Relational Provision: Jerome began facilitating family meetings where everyone could share their thoughts and feelings.

Cultural Provision: Jerome started teaching his children about their African American heritage, taking them to museums, cultural events, and family reunions.

Two Years Later: Follow-Up

Jerome now runs a mentorship program called "Holistic Fathers" that helps other Black men expand their understanding of provision. "I learned that my children needed my heart, not just my hustle," Jerome reflects. "When I started providing emotionally and spiritually, not just financially, everything changed."

His wife Keisha adds: "Jerome still works hard, but now he works smart. He provides for our whole family—our hearts, our minds, our spirits, not just our bank account. The kids are thriving because they have a father who's present in every way that matters."

Their son Marcus, now 14, says: "My dad still provides everything we need, but now I know he loves me, not just loves taking care of me. That makes all the difference."

Clinical Applications: Working with Provision-Oriented Clients

Assessment Questions:

- "What did provision look like in your family growing up? Who provided what?"

- "How do you measure whether you're being a good provider? What would need to change for you to feel successful?"

- "If money weren't an issue, how would you show love and care for your family?"

Therapeutic Interventions:

- Psychoeducation about systemic barriers to Black male economic success

- Comprehensive provision planning that includes all forms of care

- Partner education about recognizing non-financial forms of provision

- Values clarification exercises to identify what matters most beyond money

Warning Signs:

- Client equates his worth entirely with his earning capacity
- Extreme work hours that damage relationships and health
- Guilt or shame when partner earns more or when unable to provide financially
- Resistance to other forms of contribution that don't involve money

Key Takeaways from Provision as Expression:

- True provision is comprehensive care—financial, emotional, spiritual, and relational
- The system was designed to limit your economic power, then judge you for limitation
- Biblical and traditional African provision was holistic, not just financial
- Your worth is not measured by your wallet but by your willingness to give what you have

Next Steps:

- Complete a "provision audit"—assess all the ways you currently provide for your family
- Identify your unique strengths and find ways to provide through them
- Work with your partner to create a comprehensive provision plan

- Practice providing from fullness, not depletion

Reflection Questions:

- What messages did you learn about provision growing up?

- How might you be providing in ways that aren't being recognized?

- What would change if you saw provision as stewardship rather than performance?

- How can you provide sustainably without burning yourself out?

Chapter 3: Respect as Intimacy

Love Language 3

"*Respect is not about ego—it's about creating emotional safety. When a Black man feels respected, he feels safe enough to be vulnerable. When he feels disrespected, he feels unsafe enough to withdraw.*" — Dr. Shaun Harper

Opening Reflection

For many Black men, respect isn't just a preference—it's a prerequisite for emotional intimacy. We've been conditioned by a world that consistently disrespects our humanity, questions our intelligence, and challenges our authority. In environments where our competence is doubted and our character is questioned, respect becomes the foundation upon which all other forms of connection are built.

But respect as a love language is often misunderstood. It's not about ego, dominance, or control. It's about emotional safety. When a Black man feels respected, he feels safe enough to be vulnerable, to share his fears, to admit his mistakes, to ask for help. When he feels disrespected, he feels unsafe enough to withdraw, to protect himself, to shut down emotionally.

The challenge is that respect means different things to different people. What feels like respect to him might feel like distance to her. What feels like love to her might feel like disrespect to him. The key is understanding that for many Black men, respect is the gateway to intimacy, not a barrier to it.

This understanding is crucial because it reframes respect from a power dynamic to a healing dynamic. For Black men who have experienced systematic disrespect, feeling respected in intimate relationships isn't about control—it's about restoration. It's about having at least one space where their humanity is honored, their competence is acknowledged, and their contributions are valued.

The Science of Respect and Safety

When Black men feel disrespected, their nervous system activates what researchers call the "threat detection system." This system prioritizes survival over connection, making emotional vulnerability feel dangerous. Your body literally cannot access the pathways necessary for intimacy when it perceives threats to your dignity or worth.

However, when you feel genuinely respected, your nervous system can shift into what researchers call the "social engagement system"—a state where vulnerability, emotional expression, and deep connection become possible. Respect isn't just nice to have for Black men—it's a neurobiological necessity for emotional intimacy and authentic connection.

Case Study: David and Monica's Respect Disconnect - Extended Analysis

David is a 39-year-old engineer and father of two. His wife Monica is a successful marketing executive. Despite their professional success, their marriage struggles with communication and intimacy. In couples therapy, their different understandings of respect create ongoing conflict.

Monica explains: "He gets defensive about everything. If I suggest a different way to handle the kids' homework, he acts like I'm attacking his parenting. If I have an opinion about our finances, he shuts down. I feel like I have to walk on eggshells around his ego."

David responds: "She doesn't respect my judgment. She questions everything I do, corrects me in front of the kids, acts like I don't know what I'm doing. At work, people respect my expertise. At home, I feel like I can't do anything right. So I stop trying."

The Deeper Story: Respect as Survival

Through extended therapy sessions, David revealed the deeper story behind his need for respect. As one of only three Black engineers in his company, David faced constant microaggressions and challenges to his competence. Colleagues would question his ideas in meetings, then praise the same ideas when presented by white colleagues.

"Every day at work, I have to prove that I belong there," David explained. "People assume I'm less qualified, less intelligent, less capable. When I come home and Monica questions my judgment about our kids or our finances, it feels like the same thing."

David's need for respect wasn't about ego—it was about having one space where his competence was assumed rather than questioned, where his judgment was trusted rather than doubted, where his contributions were valued rather than minimized.

The Transformation Process

The healing process involved both partners learning new ways of communicating that honored each other's core needs:

David's Growth:

- **Reframing Input as Care**: David learned to interpret Monica's suggestions as expressions of care and investment rather than attacks on his competence.

- **Communicating Needs**: David learned to say, "I need to feel like you trust my judgment" instead of just getting defensive.

- **Separating Work from Home**: David began processing his work stress separately so it didn't contaminate his home relationships.

Monica's Growth:

- **Respect-Informed Communication**: Monica learned to frame suggestions in ways that honored David's competence: "You're such a good father. I have an idea about homework that might work alongside what you're already doing."

- **Affirmation Before Input**: Monica began acknowledging David's strengths before offering different perspectives.

- **Understanding Trauma**: Monica learned about the specific challenges Black men face and how that affected David's need for respect.

Two Years Later: Follow-Up

David and Monica now facilitate workshops on "Respect-Informed Communication" for couples in their community. "We learned that respect and partnership aren't opposites—they're complementary," Monica explains. "When I approach David with respect for his judgment, he's actually more open to my ideas because he doesn't feel attacked."

David adds: "I learned that Monica's input wasn't disrespect—it was investment. She cares enough about our family to share her thoughts. Now when she has suggestions, I can hear her heart instead of just hearing criticism."

Their communication has become a model for other couples. "They show us that you can disagree without being disrespectful," says their friend Marcus. "David still leads his family, but Monica is truly his partner. They both win."

Historical Context: The Systematic Disrespect of Black Manhood

To understand why respect is such a crucial love language for Black men, we must examine the historical and ongoing patterns of systematic disrespect that have shaped our experience.

From Slavery to Jim Crow: The Deliberate Emasculation

During slavery, Black men were systematically stripped of respect and authority. They were prevented from protecting their families, providing for their children, or exercising any form of leadership or decision-making power. The system was designed to break Black male dignity and reduce grown men to the status of children or property.

The Jim Crow era continued this pattern through different means. Black men were required to show deference to white authority, regardless of age, education, or accomplishment. They were called "boy" regardless of their age, denied titles of respect like "Mr." or "Sir," and expected to step aside, look down, and submit to white authority in all interactions.

Contemporary Manifestations

These historical patterns continue in contemporary forms:

Educational Disrespect: Black boys are suspended and expelled at disproportionate rates, often for the same behaviors that result in lesser consequences for other boys.

Workplace Disrespect: Black men face hiring discrimination, promotion barriers, and workplace microaggressions that question their competence and character.

Media Disrespect: Black men are consistently portrayed in media as criminals, absent fathers, or comic relief. Positive representations are rare and often one-dimensional.

Criminal Justice Disrespect: Black men are disproportionately targeted, arrested, convicted, and sentenced, creating a narrative of criminality that affects how society views all Black men.

This systematic negation creates what psychologists call "dignity deficits"—consistent experiences of disrespect that accumulate over time and create chronic stress, hypervigilance, and defensive responses that can affect all relationships.

Clinical Applications: Working with Respect-Oriented Clients

Assessment Questions:

- "Tell me about a time you felt truly respected. How did that affect your ability to be vulnerable?"

- "When you feel disrespected, what happens in your body? Your relationships?"

- "How does respect create safety for you in relationships?"

Therapeutic Interventions:

- Psychoeducation about dignity trauma and nervous system responses to disrespect

- Respect-informed communication skills training for couples

- Partner education about cultural context of respect needs for Black men
- Helping clients distinguish between respect and agreement

Warning Signs:

- Client withdraws when feeling criticized by therapist or partner
- Defensive responses to feedback or suggestions, even well-intentioned ones
- Difficulty accessing emotions when dignity feels threatened
- Escalation when client perceives disrespect, even in minor interactions

Therapeutic Stance:

- Lead with affirmation of client's strengths before addressing growth areas
- Frame treatment as collaboration, not expert-patient dynamic
- Understand that respect creates safety for deeper therapeutic work
- Honor the client's expertise about his own experience

Key Takeaways from Respect as Intimacy:

- Respect creates emotional safety that allows vulnerability and intimacy to flourish
- Your need for respect is rooted in dignity, not ego—honor that

distinction

- Partners can disagree with you while still respecting your competence and character

- Respect-informed communication leads to deeper connection, not distant relationships

Next Steps:

- Educate your partner about why respect creates safety for your vulnerability

- Be specific about what respect looks like to you in daily interactions

- Model the respect you want to receive by honoring others' dignity

- Separate respect from agreement—people can respect you while disagreeing

Reflection Questions:

- How has systematic disrespect affected your ability to be vulnerable?

- What does respect look like in your most important relationships?

- How can you communicate your need for respect without demanding or controlling?

- When do you feel most respected, and how does that affect your emotional availability?

Chapter 4: Loyalty as Language

Love Language 4

"Loyalty is not blind devotion. It's conscious choice, repeated daily, to remain committed to someone's growth and well-being even when it's difficult." — Dr. Brené Brown

Opening Reflection

In a world that has taught Black men that we are disposable, that our presence is temporary, that our commitment is conditional, loyalty becomes our most powerful declaration of love. We stay when others leave. We remain when others run. We choose consistency when others choose convenience.

But loyalty as a love language is complex. It can be our greatest strength and our deepest wound. It can be the foundation of lasting relationships or the prison that keeps us trapped in unhealthy dynamics. The difference lies in understanding the distinction between healthy loyalty—which includes boundaries, mutuality, and growth—and toxic loyalty—which demands self-abandonment, enables dysfunction, and perpetuates harm.

For many Black men, loyalty was learned in environments where leaving meant abandonment, where inconsistency meant betrayal, where commitment was the only currency we had to offer. We learned to stay not just because we loved, but because staying was how we proved we were different from those who left us.

True loyalty is not about staying no matter what—it's about being committed to someone's highest good, even when that requires difficult conversations, boundaries, or sometimes, loving them enough to let them go.

The Science of Loyalty and Attachment

Recent research helps us understand why loyalty becomes such a primary love language for many Black men. Loyalty is fundamentally about attachment security—the deep human need to know that our most important relationships are stable and dependable.

For individuals who have experienced abandonment, inconsistency, or betrayal, the nervous system develops what researchers call "hypervigilant attachment"—a heightened sensitivity to signs of abandonment or disloyalty. This creates an intense drive to prove loyalty and secure commitment from others.

However, this same drive that makes loyalty so important can also create problems when it becomes rigid or one-sided. The nervous system that developed loyalty as a survival strategy may struggle to recognize when loyalty becomes unhealthy or when boundaries are necessary for well-being.

Case Study: Kingdom and the Weight of Loyalty - Extended Analysis

Kingdom is a 35-year-old man who has been with his partner Jasmine for eight years. Despite ongoing issues with communication, intimacy, and mutual respect, Kingdom refuses to consider ending the relationship. In therapy, he explains:

"I'm not my father. I'm not going to be another Black man who walks away when things get hard. I made a commitment, and I'm going to honor it."

Jasmine responds: "But you're not really here. You're physically present, but emotionally you've checked out. You stay, but you don't engage. You're loyal to the idea of us, but not to the reality of us."

The Deeper Story: Loyalty as Identity

Through extended therapy sessions, Kingdom revealed the deeper story behind his rigid loyalty. His father had left when Kingdom was nine years old, promising to return but never coming back. His mother struggled with depression and addiction, creating an unstable home environment where Kingdom learned that his job was to stay, to be loyal, to never abandon ship no matter how difficult things became.

Kingdom's loyalty wasn't just about love—it was about identity. He had built his entire sense of self around being the man who stays, the man who doesn't abandon, the man who honors his commitments.

The Transformation Process

Kingdom's healing journey involved learning to expand his understanding of loyalty from passive endurance to active commitment:

Understanding Healthy Boundaries: Kingdom learned that loyalty doesn't mean accepting mistreatment or dysfunction. Healthy loyalty includes boundaries that protect both partners' well-being.

Engaging in Conflict: Instead of avoiding difficult conversations to maintain peace, Kingdom learned to engage in conflict as an expression of loyalty to the relationship's health.

Mutual Accountability: Kingdom learned that loyalty includes holding his partner accountable for her behavior while also being accountable for his own.

Two Years Later: Follow-Up

Kingdom and Jasmine are now married and expecting their first child. "Kingdom is still the most loyal man I know," Jasmine shares, "but now his loyalty includes fighting for our relationship, not just staying in it. He's loyal to our growth, not just our survival."

Kingdom reflects: "I learned that real loyalty means caring enough about someone to do the hard work of building a healthy relationship. It's not enough to just not leave—I have to actively love, actively engage, actively grow."

They now mentor other couples through a program called "Active Loyalty," helping partners understand the difference between healthy commitment and passive endurance.

The Loyalty Trap: When Commitment Becomes Prison

Sometimes loyalty becomes a trap where men stay committed to relationships, situations, or systems that are harmful to their well-being. This loyalty trap manifests in several ways:

Toxic Loyalty in Relationships

Enabling Dysfunction: Staying in relationships where partners engage in destructive behavior without accountability or change.

Accepting Disrespect: Remaining loyal to partners who consistently disrespect, belittle, or mistreat them because leaving would feel like abandonment.

Avoiding Conflict: Staying silent about problems or needs to maintain peace, allowing issues to fester and relationships to deteriorate.

Self-Abandonment: Sacrificing personal well-being, dreams, or values to maintain loyalty to others.

Loyalty without boundaries is not love—it's enabling. True loyalty sometimes requires us to love people enough to set limits, to hold them accountable, or even to step away when the relationship becomes harmful.

Clinical Applications: Working with Loyalty-Oriented Clients

Assessment Questions:

- "What did loyalty look like in your family growing up? What were you taught about staying vs. leaving?"

- "How do you distinguish between healthy loyalty and loyalty that might be harmful to you?"

- "What fears come up when you think about setting boundaries with people you're loyal to?"

Therapeutic Interventions:

- Psychoeducation about healthy vs. unhealthy loyalty patterns

- Boundary-setting skills training within the context of loyal relationships

- Exploring family-of-origin messages about commitment and abandonment

- Teaching active vs. passive loyalty - engagement vs. endurance

Warning Signs:

- Client stays in clearly harmful relationships out of loyalty

- Inability to set boundaries with people they care about

- Equating any boundary-setting with abandonment or betrayal
- Loyalty that requires consistent self-sacrifice without reciprocity

Key Takeaways from Loyalty as Language:

- True loyalty is active commitment to mutual growth and well-being, not passive endurance
- Healthy loyalty includes boundaries, accountability, and sometimes difficult conversations
- You can be loyal to someone's potential while refusing to enable their dysfunction
- Loyalty should be mutual—you deserve the same commitment you give

Next Steps:

- Distinguish between healthy loyalty and loyalty that enables dysfunction
- Practice engaging in conflict as an expression of loyalty to relationship health
- Set boundaries that protect your well-being while maintaining your commitments
- Communicate what loyalty means to you and ask for reciprocal commitment

Reflection Questions:

- What did you learn about loyalty from your family of origin?

- Is your loyalty active (engaging, growing, accountable) or passive (enduring, surviving)?

- Are there relationships where your loyalty has become enabling rather than loving?

- How can you be loyal to others while also being loyal to your own well-being?

Chapter 5: Sacrifice as Devotion

Love Language 5

"True sacrifice is not about giving up everything—it's about giving with intention, wisdom, and love. It's about choosing what to give and what to preserve, what to offer and what to protect." — Dr. Brené Brown

Opening Reflection

For many Black men, love is spelled S-A-C-R-I-F-I-C-E. We learned that caring means giving up, that devotion means doing without, that love means putting everyone else's needs before our own. We work extra hours to provide for our families, give up our dreams to support others' goals, and sacrifice our comfort to ensure others' security.

This isn't wrong—sacrifice can be a beautiful expression of love. But when sacrifice becomes our only love language, when giving becomes compulsive rather than chosen, when service becomes self-abandonment, it creates relationships where we are present through our labor but absent through our exhaustion.

Sacrifice as Devotion is about intentional giving that serves love rather than guilt, that comes from abundance rather than depletion, that includes wisdom about what to give and what to preserve. It's about learning that the people we love need our presence, not just our presents; our hearts, not just our hustle; our wholeness, not just our willingness to suffer.

When we give from a place of "I am enough," our giving becomes sustainable and life-giving. When we give from "I am not enough," our giving becomes depleting and resentment-building.

The Science of Sacrifice and Reward

When we sacrifice for others, our brains release oxytocin (the bonding hormone) and dopamine (the reward chemical), creating a neurobiological reinforcement for sacrificial behavior. This explains why sacrifice can feel so meaningful and why it can also become addictive.

However, when sacrifice becomes compulsive or one-sided, it can lead to what researchers call "compassion fatigue"—a state where the reward systems become depleted, leading to exhaustion, resentment, and emotional withdrawal.

Black men often develop compulsive sacrifice as a response to historical trauma. The nervous system learns that giving is survival, that sacrifice is safety, that suffering proves worth. But this same pattern can lead to burnout and resentment when it becomes the only way to express love.

Case Study: Jamal's Journey from Martyrdom to Mindful Sacrifice

Jamal, a 37-year-old single father, worked three jobs to provide for his 12-year-old son Marcus. He rarely slept more than five hours a night, had no social life, and hadn't taken a vacation in four years. When Marcus began acting out at school, Jamal was confused and hurt.

"I give him everything," Jamal explained to his therapist. "I work myself to death to make sure he has what he needs. I sacrifice everything for him. Why is he acting like this?"

The Hidden Cost of Compulsive Sacrifice

Through therapy, Jamal discovered that his sacrifices were creating the opposite of what he intended. Marcus didn't feel loved—he felt guilty. He didn't feel provided for—he felt responsible for his father's exhaustion.

"Dad is always tired because of me," Marcus explained in a family session. "He works all the time to pay for my stuff. I wish he would just spend time with me instead of buying me things."

The Transformation Process

Jamal's healing journey involved learning to distinguish between healthy sacrifice and compulsive martyrdom:

Understanding Motivations: Jamal learned to recognize when his sacrifice was driven by love versus when it was driven by guilt, fear, or trauma.

Balancing Giving and Receiving: Jamal began to understand that healthy relationships require reciprocity, even between parents and children.

Quality over Quantity: Jamal learned that Marcus needed his presence and attention more than his presents and provisions.

Sustainable Service: Jamal developed practices that allowed him to give from fullness rather than depletion.

Two Years Later: Follow-Up

Jamal now runs a support group for single fathers called "Sustainable Sacrifice." "I learned that my greatest sacrifice wasn't my time or money—it was my willingness to be vulnerable and emotionally available," he reflects.

Marcus, now 14, says: "Dad still works hard, but now when he's home, he's really home. We talk, we play games, we watch movies. I don't feel guilty anymore because I can see that he's happy, not just tired."

Jamal has become a model in their community for sustainable parenting. "I provide for Marcus financially, emotionally, and spiritually now," he explains. "He gets my whole heart, not just my hustle."

The Martyr Complex: When Sacrifice Becomes Self-Abandonment

Many Black men develop what therapists call a "martyr complex"—the unconscious belief that love requires self-abandonment, that caring means suffering, that being a good man means being a tired man.

This isn't love—it's trauma masquerading as virtue. It's the wound of never feeling worthy unless you're giving, never feeling valuable unless you're suffering.

Characteristics of the Martyr Complex:

Compulsive Giving: Feeling unable to say no to requests for help, time, or resources, even when giving would be harmful to your well-being.

Guilt About Self-Care: Feeling selfish or guilty when prioritizing your own needs, rest, or pleasure.

Worth Through Suffering: Believing that your value is measured by how much you sacrifice or how much you suffer for others.

Resentment Building: Feeling angry or bitter when your sacrifices are not appreciated or reciprocated, but continuing to give anyway.

The martyr complex often develops as a response to childhood trauma or neglect. The child learns that the only way to secure love and attention is through giving, serving, and sacrificing. This pattern continues into adulthood, creating relationships where the person gives everything but receives little.

Clinical Applications: Working with Sacrifice-Oriented Clients

Assessment Questions:

- "Tell me about how sacrifice was modeled in your family growing up."

- "What drives your desire to give and serve others? What would happen if you stopped?"

- "When you give to others, what are you hoping to receive in return?"

Therapeutic Interventions:

- Psychoeducation about healthy vs. compulsive giving patterns
- Boundary-setting skills training to prevent burnout and resentment
- Values clarification to distinguish between chosen sacrifice and obligated sacrifice
- Self-care planning that frames personal well-being as responsibility, not selfishness

Warning Signs:

- Client works excessive hours at expense of health and relationships
- Inability to say no to requests for help, even unreasonable ones
- Guilt or shame when taking time for personal needs or pleasure
- Resentment toward those they serve, but continued compulsive giving

Key Takeaways from Sacrifice as Devotion:

- Healthy sacrifice comes from abundance, not depletion—you can't give what you don't have
- Your worth is not measured by your willingness to suffer, but by your wisdom in giving

- Sustainable sacrifice includes self-care, boundaries, and reciprocity

- The people you love need your wholeness, not your willingness to be depleted

Next Steps:

- Distinguish between chosen sacrifice and compulsive martyrdom in your relationships

- Set boundaries around your giving to ensure sustainability

- Practice receiving as well as giving in your important relationships

- Reframe self-care as stewardship, not selfishness

Reflection Questions:

- What motivates your sacrifice—love, guilt, fear, or obligation?

- Are you sacrificing from fullness or from depletion?

- What would change if you gave from choice rather than compulsion?

- How can you serve others without abandoning yourself?

Chapter 6: Affirmation as Healing

Love Language 6

"Affirmation is not about inflating ego—it's about healing wounds. For Black men who have faced systematic negation, genuine affirmation becomes a form of medicine that restores dignity, worth, and hope." — Dr. Thema Bryant

Opening Reflection

For many Black men, affirmation isn't just nice to hear—it's necessary for healing. We've grown up in a world that consistently tells us we're too much or not enough, too aggressive or too passive, too confident or too insecure. We've faced systematic criticism, microaggressions, and negative stereotypes that attack our character, question our competence, and diminish our worth.

In this context, genuine affirmation becomes more than encouragement—it becomes medicine. It's the antidote to internalized oppression, the healing balm for wounded dignity, the restoration of worth that society has tried to strip away. When someone sees our character, acknowledges our efforts, and speaks life into our potential, they're not just being nice—they're participating in our healing.

But affirmation as a love language is often misunderstood. It's not about ego stroking or false praise. It's not about avoiding accountability or enabling dysfunction. True affirmation recognizes genuine character, acknowledges real effort, and speaks truth about potential and worth. It's about seeing and naming the good that exists, even when it's buried under pain, trauma, or defensive behaviors.

For individuals who have experienced systematic devaluation, affirmation is not luxury—it's necessity. The brain that has been consistently told it's worthless needs consistent messages of worth to heal and thrive.

The Science of Affirmation and Healing

Recent research in neuroscience reveals why affirmation is so powerful for healing trauma and building resilience. The brain has a "negativity bias"—it's wired to notice and remember negative experiences more than positive ones.

This negativity bias served our ancestors well when survival depended on quickly identifying and remembering threats. However, for individuals who have experienced chronic criticism, discrimination, or trauma, this bias can become problematic, creating a mental environment where negative messages are easily absorbed while positive messages are dismissed or forgotten.

The brain is like Velcro for negative experiences and Teflon for positive ones. For individuals who have experienced chronic criticism or trauma, intentional affirmation can literally rewire the brain to notice and internalize positive experiences.

For Black men, this neurobiological understanding is particularly important. Systematic discrimination creates chronic stress in the nervous system, leading to hypervigilance, defensive responses, and difficulty receiving positive feedback.

However, consistent, genuine affirmation can help heal these neurobiological patterns. When Black men receive regular, specific affirmation, several positive changes occur in the brain:

- Reduced hypervigilance and defensive reactions

- Increased self-esteem and confidence

- Improved emotional regulation and stress management

- Enhanced relationship satisfaction and intimacy

- Decreased symptoms of depression and anxiety

Case Study: Anthony and Simone - From Criticism to Affirmation

Anthony, a 33-year-old accountant, and Simone, a 31-year-old nurse, had been married for six years but struggled with communication patterns that left both feeling frustrated and disconnected. Anthony felt constantly criticized and unappreciated, while Simone felt like Anthony was defensive and unwilling to grow.

The Criticism Cycle

Their typical interaction pattern looked like this:
- Simone would notice something she wanted Anthony to change or improve
- She would point out the problem, often focusing on what was wrong
- Anthony would feel criticized and become defensive
- Simone would feel unheard and increase her intensity
- Anthony would withdraw or counterattack
- Both would feel hurt and misunderstood

"I feel like nothing I do is ever good enough," Anthony explained in therapy. "She always has something to say about how I could do better, but she never acknowledges what I'm already doing right."

The Transformation Process

Their therapist introduced Anthony and Simone to the concept of "affirmation-first communication"—an approach that prioritizes recognition and appreciation while still allowing for growth and feedback.

For Simone:
- **Affirmation Before Feedback**: Starting conversations by acknowledging Anthony's strengths and efforts before addressing areas for growth

- **Specific Recognition**: Offering detailed, specific affirmation rather than generic praise

- **Character Focus**: Recognizing Anthony's character and intentions, not just his actions

For Anthony:
- **Receiving Practice**: Learning to accept and internalize affirmation rather than dismissing it

- **Feedback Openness**: Understanding that Simone's feedback came from love, not criticism

- **Self-Affirmation**: Developing the ability to recognize and appreciate his own efforts and growth

Two Years Later: Follow-Up

Anthony and Simone now facilitate communication workshops called "Affirmation First" at their church. "When I start with affirmation, Anthony is so much more open to feedback," Simone explains. "He doesn't get defensive because he knows I see and appreciate the good in him."

Anthony adds: "Now when Simone wants to talk about something, she might start by saying, 'I love how hard you work for our family. I have an idea about something that might help us even more.' That feels completely different than being told what I'm doing wrong."

Their marriage has become a model for other couples struggling with criticism cycles. "They show us that you can have high standards without being critical," says their friend David. "Affirmation makes growth feel safe instead of threatening."

The Healing Power of Specific Affirmation

Not all affirmation is created equal. Generic praise like "good job" or "you're great" doesn't have the same healing power as specific affirmation that recognizes character, effort, and growth.

Elements of Healing Affirmation:

Character Recognition: "I see your integrity in how you handle difficult situations." This type of affirmation recognizes the person's moral character and values, countering messages that Black men are untrustworthy or lacking in character.

Effort Appreciation: "I notice how hard you work to provide for our family." This acknowledges the sacrifice and dedication involved in the person's efforts, countering messages that Black men are lazy or irresponsible.

Growth Acknowledgment: "I'm proud of how you've grown in expressing your emotions." This recognizes progress and development, countering messages that Black men are incapable of change or growth.

Impact Awareness: "Your presence makes me feel safe and loved." This acknowledges the positive effect the person has on others, countering messages that Black men are dangerous or harmful.

Potential Belief: "I believe in your ability to achieve your dreams." This expresses confidence in the person's capabilities and future, countering messages that Black men have limited potential.

Value Declaration: "You matter to me and to this family." This affirms the person's inherent worth and importance, countering messages that Black men are disposable or unimportant.

Specific affirmation works because it provides concrete evidence against internalized negative beliefs. When someone specifically names your character, effort, or impact, it becomes harder to dismiss or minimize.

Clinical Applications: Working with Affirmation-Oriented Clients

Assessment Questions:

- "What kind of feedback did you receive growing up? How did people acknowledge your efforts or character?"

- "What type of affirmation feels most meaningful to you? What makes you feel truly seen and appreciated?"

- "How do you typically respond when someone gives you a compliment or acknowledges your efforts?"

Therapeutic Interventions:

- Psychoeducation about the neurobiological impact of affirmation on trauma recovery

- Teaching clients to identify and internalize genuine affirmation

- Partner training on giving specific, meaningful affirmation vs. generic praise

- Cognitive restructuring to counter negative self-talk with affirming self-statements

Warning Signs:

- Client consistently deflects or dismisses positive feedback

- Inability to acknowledge own strengths or accomplishments

- Extreme sensitivity to criticism combined with hunger for affirmation

- Using achievements to seek affirmation rather than expressing authentic self

Key Takeaways from Affirmation as Healing:

- Affirmation is medicine for the Black male psyche that has faced systematic negation

- Specific affirmation that names character, effort, and impact is more healing than generic praise

- Your need for affirmation isn't weakness—it's the natural response to a lifetime of criticism

- You can learn to receive affirmation gracefully while also offering it authentically to others

Next Steps:

- Practice saying "thank you" instead of dismissing compliments
- Ask trusted people to give you specific feedback about your character and impact
- Keep a record of affirmations you receive to review during difficult times
- Look for opportunities to offer genuine, specific affirmation to others

Reflection Questions:

- What messages about yourself have you internalized from a lifetime of criticism?
- How does receiving genuine affirmation affect your ability to be vulnerable?
- What specific types of affirmation feel most healing to you?
- How can you create more affirmation-rich relationships in your life?

Chapter 7: Touch as Trust

Love Language 7

"Touch is the first language we learn and the last one we forget. For Black men who have been taught that physical affection is weakness, reclaiming touch is reclaiming a fundamental part of our humanity." — Dr. Bessel van der Kolk

Opening Reflection

For many Black men, physical touch exists in a complicated space between desire and danger, between healing and harm, between connection and vulnerability. We've been taught that real men don't need physical affection, that touch is either sexual or weak, that physical comfort is something we provide but don't receive.

But touch is one of our most fundamental human needs. It's how we first experienced love in the womb, how we were comforted as children, how we learned that we were safe and valued. Touch releases oxytocin, reduces stress hormones, lowers blood pressure, and creates bonds that words alone cannot forge. When we deny ourselves this basic human need, we deny ourselves a powerful source of healing and connection.

Touch as Trust is about reclaiming physical affection as a legitimate love language—one that includes everything from a supportive hand on the shoulder to intimate physical connection. It's about learning that touch can be healing rather than harmful, connecting rather than controlling, nurturing rather than needy.

Touch is not luxury—it's necessity. The body that has been traumatized needs safe, healing touch to remember that it can be held without being hurt, that it can be vulnerable without being violated.

The Science of Touch and Healing

Recent research in neuroscience reveals the profound impact that touch has on our physical and emotional well-being. Appropriate touch triggers the release of oxytocin (the bonding hormone), reduces cortisol (the stress hormone), and activates the parasympathetic nervous system (the rest and digest response).

For individuals who have experienced trauma, these neurobiological effects are particularly important. Trauma often leaves the nervous system in a state of hypervigilance, where the body is constantly scanning for threat and preparing for danger. Safe, consensual touch can help regulate this dysregulated nervous system, signaling safety and promoting healing.

Safe touch activates the ventral vagal complex, which is associated with social engagement, calm, and connection. This is why appropriate touch can be so healing for trauma survivors—it literally helps the nervous system remember how to feel safe.

For Black men, who often carry trauma from experiences of racism, violence, and emotional neglect, understanding the neuroscience of touch is crucial. Touch is not just about physical pleasure or emotional connection—it's about nervous system regulation and trauma healing.

Case Study: Kevin's Journey from Touch Avoidance to Touch Healing

Kevin, a 39-year-old engineer, came to therapy because his wife Lisa was threatening to leave him over his inability to be physically affectionate. "He never touches me unless he wants sex," Lisa explained. "I need hugs, hand-holding, cuddling—just physical connection that isn't about sex. But he acts like I'm asking for something weird."

Kevin's response revealed the complexity of his relationship with touch: "I don't know how to do that stuff. It feels awkward and uncomfortable. I wasn't raised with a lot of hugging and touching. And honestly, when she wants to cuddle or hold hands, I don't know what she wants from me."

The Deeper Story: Touch and Trauma

Through therapy, Kevin revealed the deeper story behind his touch avoidance. He had grown up in a household where physical affection was rare and physical violence was common. His father was emotionally distant and physically harsh, using physical punishment as the primary form of discipline.

"The only time my father touched me was to hit me," Kevin shared. "And my mother was so overwhelmed and stressed that she didn't have time for hugs or cuddling. I learned that touch meant pain or that it was something you didn't have time for."

Kevin's experience was compounded by cultural messages about Black masculinity that discouraged physical affection between men and portrayed emotional vulnerability as weakness.

The Healing Process

Kevin's journey toward reclaiming touch as a love language involved several stages of healing and growth:

Understanding His History: Kevin learned to recognize how his childhood experiences and cultural messages had shaped his relationship with touch.

Trauma Healing: Kevin worked with a trauma specialist to heal the wounds that made touch feel dangerous or uncomfortable.

Nervous System Regulation: Kevin learned techniques for calming his nervous system and creating safety in his body.

Gradual Exposure: Kevin began practicing small acts of physical affection, starting with brief touches and gradually building to longer, more intimate contact.

Two Years Later: Follow-Up

Kevin and Lisa now teach workshops on "Reclaiming Touch" for couples in their community. "Learning to touch and be touched has changed everything for me," Kevin reflects. "I didn't realize how much I was missing by avoiding physical affection. Now when Lisa and I cuddle or hold hands, I feel connected to her in a way I never experienced before."

Lisa adds: "Kevin is like a different person. He initiates hugs, he holds my hand when we're walking, he cuddles with me while we watch TV. I feel loved and wanted in a way I never did before. And the amazing thing is that our sexual connection has improved too because we have more physical intimacy overall."

Their transformation has impacted their children as well. "Dad hugs us now," says their 10-year-old daughter Sarah. "It makes me feel safe and loved. I used to think he didn't like hugs, but now I know he was just learning how."

The Touch Deprivation Crisis

Many Black men suffer from what researchers call "touch deprivation"—a lack of appropriate physical affection that can have serious consequences for physical and emotional health. Touch deprivation can lead to:

- Increased stress and anxiety

- Weakened immune system

- Higher blood pressure

- Difficulty with emotional regulation

- Problems with social connection

- Increased aggression and irritability
- Depression and loneliness

For Black men, touch deprivation is often compounded by cultural messages that discourage physical affection and historical trauma that makes touch feel unsafe.

The Masculine Touch Deficit

Traditional masculine socialization often creates what researchers call a "touch deficit" for men. Boys are taught early that physical affection is feminine, that real men don't need comfort, and that touch should be limited to sexual contexts or aggressive competition.

Boys learn to suppress their need for physical affection and emotional intimacy, creating a deficit that affects their relationships throughout their lives. They become touch-starved and emotionally isolated.

For Black men, this masculine touch deficit is often intensified by additional cultural pressures around strength, independence, and emotional control.

The Spectrum of Healing Touch

Touch as Trust encompasses a wide spectrum of physical affection, from the most casual to the most intimate. Understanding this spectrum helps Black men and their partners navigate physical affection in ways that feel safe and comfortable for everyone.

Types of Healing Touch:

Casual Touch: Brief, friendly physical contact like handshakes, fist bumps, or pats on the back. This type of touch builds comfort with physical contact and creates social connection.

Comfort Touch: Physical affection offered during times of stress or sadness, like a hand on the shoulder or a supportive hug. This touch provides emotional support and communicates care.

Affectionate Touch: Regular physical expressions of love like holding hands, hugging, or cuddling. This touch builds emotional intimacy and strengthens relationship bonds.

Therapeutic Touch: Intentional touch for healing purposes, like massage, gentle stretching, or other forms of bodywork. This touch promotes physical and emotional healing.

Intimate Touch: Deeper physical connection that may or may not be sexual, like extended cuddling, caressing, or massage between partners. This touch creates deep emotional and physical intimacy.

The key is understanding that each level of touch serves different emotional needs and requires different levels of trust and consent. Black men can learn to give and receive touch at all levels while maintaining appropriate boundaries and respect for others' comfort.

Clinical Applications: Working with Touch-Oriented Clients

Assessment Questions:

- "What was physical affection like in your family growing up? How did people show care through touch?"

- "What makes physical touch feel safe vs. threatening for you?"

- "How do you currently express care through physical affection, and how would you like to grow in this area?"

Therapeutic Interventions:

- Trauma-informed approach to addressing touch avoidance or touch trauma

- Gradual exposure exercises for increasing comfort with appropriate physical affection

- Partner education about the importance of consensual, healing touch

- Nervous system regulation techniques to create safety for physical intimacy

Warning Signs:

- Complete avoidance of physical touch, even casual or comfort touch

- Touch that feels compulsive or is used to avoid emotional intimacy

- Inability to set boundaries around unwanted touch

- Touch trauma that requires specialized treatment

Therapeutic Stance:

- Never pressure clients toward physical touch - always follow their lead and pace

- Understand that touch avoidance may be trauma-informed and protective

- Frame touch as one of many love languages, not a requirement for healthy relationships

- Address underlying trauma before working on increasing physical affection

Key Takeaways from Touch as Trust:

- Physical touch is a basic human need that supports both physical and emotional well-being

- Touch avoidance is often trauma-informed—healing the trauma can restore comfort with touch

- Healthy touch exists on a spectrum from casual to intimate, all serving different emotional needs

- Reclaiming appropriate touch is reclaiming a fundamental part of your humanity

Next Steps:

- Start with self-touch—massage, gentle stretching, or other self-care practices

- Practice gradual exposure to casual and comfort touch with safe people

- Communicate with your partner about your touch journey and what feels safe

- Address any trauma that makes touch feel threatening through therapy or healing work

Reflection Questions:

- What messages did you learn about physical affection growing up?
- How do those messages serve you now, and how do they limit you?
- What would it mean to be more comfortable with appropriate touch?
- How can you heal from any trauma that makes touch difficult?

Chapter 8: Love Language Fluency

Integration and Growth

"Fluency isn't about perfection—it's about flexibility. The goal isn't to master every love language, but to expand your emotional vocabulary so you can connect more deeply with the people you care about." — Michael Darby

Understanding Your Love Language Profile

Just as people have different learning styles, Black men have different love language preferences. While you may have one primary love language, you likely have a combination that reflects your unique personality, experiences, and relationships.

Creating Your Love Language Profile

Your love language profile might look something like this:

Primary Love Language: Respect as Intimacy (40%) **Secondary Love Language**: Provision as Expression (25%) **Tertiary Love Languages**: Presence as Protection (15%), Loyalty as Language (10%), Sacrifice as Devotion (5%), Affirmation as Healing (3%), Touch as Trust (2%)

This doesn't mean you only need respect and provision. It means these are your most natural ways of expressing and receiving love, while the others are areas where you can grow and expand.

The Raw and Refined Spectrum

Remember, each love language exists on a spectrum from raw to refined:

Raw Expression: Authentic but shaped by trauma and survival. For example, raw Presence as Protection might be silent endurance, while raw Sacrifice as Devotion might be compulsive martyrdom.

Refined Expression: That same authentic love, processed through healing and growth. Refined Presence as Protection becomes emotionally engaged availability, while refined Sacrifice as Devotion becomes intentional, sustainable service.

The goal isn't to eliminate the raw expression—it's to refine it through healing, communication, and growth.

When Love Languages Conflict

What happens when your primary love language is Respect as Intimacy, but your partner's primary need is for verbal affirmation? Or when you express love through Sacrifice as Devotion, but your partner experiences that as emotional distance?

The Translation Process

Love language conflicts aren't relationship failures—they're translation opportunities. Here's how to navigate them:

Step 1: Recognize the Love Being Offered Before asking for what you need, acknowledge the love being given in a different language. "I see that you're working extra hours to provide for us. That tells me you love us."

Step 2: Translate Your Needs Help your partner understand your love language without criticizing theirs. "I feel most loved when you acknowledge my efforts and treat me with respect. Can you help me with that?"

Step 3: Learn Their Language Ask your partner what makes them feel most loved and practice expressing love in their language. "What helps you feel most connected to me?"

Step 4: Create Bilingual Love Build relationships where both love languages are spoken fluently. You don't have to abandon your natural way of loving—you just need to expand it.

Example: Respect Meets Affirmation

Marcus expresses love through Respect as Intimacy—he honors his wife's decisions, trusts her judgment, and creates space for her leadership in areas where she excels. But Keisha feels most loved through Affirmation as Healing—she needs to hear words that acknowledge her efforts and character.

The Conflict: Marcus shows respect by not commenting on Keisha's parenting choices, thinking that silence shows trust. Keisha interprets this silence as lack of interest or appreciation.

The Translation: Marcus learns to combine respect with affirmation: "I love watching you with the kids. You're such a wise mother, and I trust your instincts completely." This honors both his need to show respect and her need to receive affirmation.

Building Love Language Fluency Over Time

Becoming fluent in love languages is like learning any new skill—it takes practice, patience, and persistence.

The 30-60-90 Day Growth Plan

First 30 Days: Assessment and Awareness
- Take the Love Language Assessment (see Appendix)
- Share your primary love language with your partner and family

- Practice recognizing when others express love in different languages
- Begin one daily practice from your primary love language chapter

Days 31-60: Expansion and Practice
- Choose one secondary love language to develop
- Practice expressing love in your partner's primary language daily
- Address any trauma or barriers that limit your love language expression
- Join or create a support group focused on emotional growth

Days 61-90: Integration and Refinement
- Evaluate your growth and adjust your practices
- Teach someone else about the 7 Love Languages framework
- Plan for long-term growth and development
- Celebrate the progress you've made

Long-Term Fluency Development

Year 1: Foundation Building Focus on mastering your primary love language while learning to recognize and appreciate others' languages.

Year 2: Expansion and Growth Develop competency in 2-3 additional love languages, particularly those of your closest relationships.

Year 3: Teaching and Mentoring Help other Black men discover and develop their love languages. Teaching others deepens your own understanding.

Ongoing: Refinement and Evolution Continue growing in emotional intelligence, healing from trauma, and expanding your capacity for authentic love.

Love Language Assessment

Quick Assessment Tool

For each statement, rate how much it resonates with you (1 = not at all, 5 = completely):

Presence as Protection
- I show love by being consistently available and reliable
- I feel most loved when someone chooses to spend time with me
- My presence in difficult situations is how I express care
- I demonstrate commitment by showing up, even when it's hard

Provision as Expression
- I express love by taking care of people's needs
- I feel valued when people appreciate what I do for them
- Working hard for my family is how I show I care
- I measure my love by what I'm willing to give or sacrifice

Respect as Intimacy
- I need to feel respected before I can be vulnerable
- I show love by honoring others' judgment and autonomy
- Feeling trusted and valued is essential for my emotional openness
- I withdraw when I feel disrespected or criticized

Loyalty as Language
- I demonstrate love through consistent commitment
- Staying power and faithfulness are how I express devotion
- I feel most secure in relationships with mutual loyalty
- I show care by being dependable and trustworthy

Sacrifice as Devotion
- I express love by putting others' needs before my own
- Giving up things for people I care about feels natural
- I measure love by willingness to sacrifice for each other
- Service and selflessness are how I show I care

Affirmation as Healing
- I need verbal recognition and appreciation to feel valued
- Words of encouragement and praise are essential for my growth
- I express love by acknowledging others' character and efforts
- Criticism affects me deeply, while affirmation energizes me

Touch as Trust
- Physical affection is important for feeling connected
- I express care through appropriate physical touch
- Non-sexual touch helps me feel safe and loved
- Physical closeness is how I both give and receive comfort

Scoring Your Assessment

Add up your scores for each love language. Your highest score is likely your primary love language, with the next highest being your secondary languages.

Creating Love Language-Rich Relationships

For Romantic Relationships

Daily Practices:
- Morning: "How can I love you in your language today?"
- Evening: "How did I see you express love today?"
- Weekly: Love language check-in and appreciation

Monthly Practices:
- Love language date night focused on each partner's primary language
- Assessment of growth and areas for improvement
- Planning new ways to express love in each other's languages

For Father-Child Relationships

Adapting Love Languages for Children:
- **Presence**: Being available during important moments, active listening
- **Provision**: Meeting needs while teaching responsibility
- **Respect**: Honoring their growing autonomy and individual personality

- **Loyalty**: Consistency in your love regardless of their behavior

- **Sacrifice**: Investing time and energy in their growth and development

- **Affirmation**: Specific praise for character and effort, not just achievement

- **Touch**: Appropriate physical affection that communicates safety and love

For Friendships and Brotherhood

Building Love Language Community:
- Create spaces where Black men can practice vulnerability and emotional expression

- Form accountability partnerships focused on emotional growth

- Develop mentorship relationships that model healthy love language expression

- Support each other in healing trauma that limits love language development

Overcoming Common Obstacles

"This Feels Too Soft"

Many Black men worry that developing emotional intelligence and love language fluency will make them weak or feminine. Remember:
- Emotional intelligence is a form of strength, not weakness

- The strongest men are those who can be both powerful and tender

- Your ancestors were emotionally expressive before trauma and oppression taught you otherwise

- Growing in love languages expands your influence and impact

"My Partner Doesn't Understand"

If your partner struggles to understand your love languages:
- Lead with patience—this is new for them too

- Share this book and discuss it together

- Model the understanding you want to receive

- Seek couples counseling with a culturally competent therapist

"I Don't Have Time for All This"

Building love language fluency doesn't require extra time—it requires intentional attention to how you're already spending your time:
- Transform existing activities by adding emotional engagement

- Practice love languages during routine interactions

- Focus on quality over quantity in your relational investments

- Remember that neglecting relationships costs more time in the long run

The Ripple Effect: Beyond Your Immediate Relationships

When you develop love language fluency, the impact extends far beyond your romantic relationship:

Your Children: They learn emotional intelligence and healthy relationship skills by watching you.

Your Community: You become a model of healthy Black masculinity for other men.

Your Legacy: You break generational cycles of emotional suppression and relational dysfunction.

Your Professional Life: Emotional intelligence and relationship skills enhance your leadership and career success.

Your Mental Health: Expressing and receiving love in multiple languages improves your overall well-being.

Key Takeaways from Love Language Fluency:

- Fluency means flexibility—expanding your emotional vocabulary to connect more deeply

- You don't have to abandon your natural love language—just expand it through healing and growth

- Love language conflicts are translation opportunities, not relationship failures

- Building fluency is a lifelong journey that benefits every area of your life

Next Steps:

- Complete the Love Language Assessment to identify your profile
- Share your results with your most important relationships
- Choose one new love language to develop over the next 90 days
- Find or create community with other men working on emotional growth

Reflection Questions:

- How has understanding love languages changed your perspective on your relationships?
- What would be possible if you became fluent in multiple love languages?
- Which love language feels most challenging for you to develop, and why?
- How can you use your love language fluency to help other Black men grow?

Chapter 9: Into Me See - A Black Man's Declaration

"The most powerful thing you can do is to be yourself in a world that is constantly trying to make you something else." — Ralph Waldo Emerson

Opening Reflection

INTO ME SEE. Intimacy. The courage to be seen, known, and loved in your full humanity. For Black men, this courage has been systematically discouraged, culturally suppressed, and personally costly. We've been taught that being seen fully is dangerous, that being known completely is weakness, that being loved authentically is impossible.

But intimacy—real intimacy—is not just about romantic relationships. It's about the courage to be your authentic self in all your relationships. It's about allowing people to see your fears and your dreams, your struggles and your triumphs, your wounds and your healing. It's about refusing to hide behind masks that protect you but also isolate you.

This final chapter is not just a conclusion—it's a declaration. A collective vow for Black men to claim healing, redefine masculinity, and walk forward in truth and grace. It's a manifesto for emotional liberation that honors where we've been while pointing toward where we can go.

The Journey We've Taken Together

Through these pages, we've explored seven love languages that reflect the unique emotional landscape of Black men:

Presence as Protection: We learned that showing up is revolutionary, but showing up with emotional engagement is transformational.

Provision as Expression: We discovered that comprehensive care goes far beyond financial support to include emotional, spiritual, and relational provision.

Respect as Intimacy: We understood that respect creates the emotional safety necessary for vulnerability and deep connection.

Loyalty as Language: We explored how commitment can be both our greatest strength and our deepest wound, depending on whether it includes growth and mutuality.

Sacrifice as Devotion: We learned to give from fullness rather than depletion, to serve without self-erasure, to love sustainably.

Affirmation as Healing: We discovered that words have power to heal wounds carved by a society that profits from our self-doubt.

Touch as Trust: We reclaimed the healing power of safe, appropriate physical affection as an expression of love and comfort.

Each of these love languages represents not just how we express love, but how we can heal from the trauma that has shaped our capacity to love. Each represents a pathway from survival to thriving, from protection to connection, from isolation to intimacy.

But there's one more language—the ultimate love language that makes all others possible: **INTO ME SEE**—the courage to be fully seen and to fully see others.

The Declaration: Who We Are and Who We're Becoming

This is our declaration—not just as individuals, but as a collective of Black men committed to emotional liberation and authentic love:

We declare that we are not broken. We are wounded warriors who have survived systems designed to destroy us. Our scars are evidence of our strength, not proof of our weakness. Our healing is not just personal—it's political, cultural, and spiritual.

We declare that we are not emotionally deficient. We have been speaking love languages that the world refused to recognize. We have been expressing care in ways that were shaped by survival but can be refined through healing. We are not learning to love—we are learning to love more fully.

We declare that we are not disposable. In a world that has treated us as expendable, we choose to see ourselves as essential. Our presence matters. Our voices matter. Our healing matters. Our love matters.

We declare that vulnerability is strength. We reject the lie that real men don't cry, don't feel, don't need help. We embrace the truth that courage includes the willingness to be seen, known, and supported in our full humanity.

We declare that we deserve love. Not love that we have to earn through performance, provision, or perfection. Love that recognizes our inherent worth, celebrates our authentic selves, and supports our continued growth.

We declare that we are worthy of healing. We refuse to accept trauma as our permanent identity. We choose therapy, growth, and transformation. We choose to break cycles rather than repeat them.

We declare that we can redefine masculinity. We reject toxic masculinity that demands emotional suppression and relational dominance. We embrace healthy masculinity that includes emotional intelligence, relational skills, and collaborative leadership.

We declare that we are not our fathers' limitations. We honor the men who raised us while choosing to expand beyond their emotional constraints. We can be both strong and soft, both protective and vulnerable, both leaders and learners.

We declare that we are not alone. We reject the lie of rugged individualism that tells us we must handle everything ourselves. We choose community, support, and mutual aid. We choose to heal together.

We declare that our love is revolutionary. In a world that has tried to break our capacity to love, choosing to love fully is an act of resistance. Our healthy relationships are a form of liberation. Our emotional growth is a form of activism.

The Manifesto: Our Collective Voice

As we stand at the threshold of this new understanding, we need more than individual declarations—we need a collective manifesto that speaks to the depths of our experience and the heights of our potential. This manifesto is not just about who we are, but about who we're becoming. It's about claiming our right to be seen, understood, and celebrated in our full humanity.

INTO ME SEE: A Black Man's Declaration

We claim the right to "Into Me See" - to look deeply within ourselves, beyond the darkened mirrors America holds up to our faces, beyond the distorted reflections forced upon us through generations of survival, beyond the calloused hands and pressed shirts that masked our fathers' pain, into the possibilities our children deserve to inherit.

Like the apostle who declared "Not that I have apprehended, but I press toward the mark," We too are men on a journey Not perfect, but purposeful like jazz through discord Not complete, but committed like grandma's steady prayers Not finished, but faithful to our growth Not bounded by our fathers' wounds But building bridges to our children's healing

[SOVEREIGN RIGHTS]

We declare our sovereign right to reject: The opinions of those who've never felt the weight of our crown The judgment of those who fear our evolution The criticism flowing from mouths that never tasted our bitter cup The expectations of those who deny our growth The limitations inherited from generations of survival The chains forged from centuries of forced stillness

[PROCLAMATION]

We proclaim: That your distance from our experience From our soul food Sundays and barbershop wisdom Disqualifies you from directing our journey That your theoretical understanding of our struggle Grants you no authority over our growth That your comfort with our compliance Cannot contain our evolution

[SACRED RIGHTS]

We declare: That we have the right to pause - Like the deep breath before a father first holds his child Not as weakness, but as wisdom passed down Not as failure, but as foundation for future generations For in this pause lies the sacred space where we can finally hear our own heartbeat, Echoing with the rhythms of ancestors and the possibilities of descendants

That we have the right to time - Time to unlearn what was forced upon our bloodline Time to remember what was stolen from our ancestors Time to discover what lies within our DNA Time to heal wounds deep as delta soil Time to build what our children will need Time to grow beyond survival into thriving

That we have the right to grace - Grace to stumble as we find our footing on paths never walked Grace to question what generations accepted as absolute Grace to feel what our fathers had to suppress Grace to heal what our grandfathers couldn't name Grace to become what our great-grandfathers couldn't dream

[REJECTION OF JUDGMENT]

We reject the snapshot judgments That freeze our stories mid-stride That ignore the miles these Jordans have walked That deny the heights we're climbing Past broken elevators in project buildings That dismiss the futures we're building In cipher circles and corner store confessionals

[SACRED QUESTIONS]

For who among you can judge a river By standing at a single bend? Who can guide me down waters You've never navigated? Who can measure an odyssey By witnessing a single step? Who can count the stars By wishing only on the falling? Who can understand our story By reading a single page When so many of those pages Lie at the bottom of the sea? Who can fathom our journey When it spans generations?

[DECLARATION OF GROWTH]

We assert our right to grow: Beyond the trauma our fathers inherited Beyond the masks our grandfathers wore Beyond the silence our great-grandfathers maintained Beyond the limitations our ancestors were forced to accept

[EVOLUTION]

We claim the sacred right of evolution: To transform past pain into future power To turn generational trauma into generational triumph To translate inherited survival into inherited thriving To transmute ancient wounds into eternal wisdom

[ANCESTRAL POWER]

For we are not just men in motion We are generations in healing We are centuries in uprising We are millennia in awakening We are ancestral dreams taking form We are future hopes made flesh

[TESTIMONY]

Let it be known: We claim the time to discover Not just for ourselves But for those who came before And those who come after

We stand firm in this truth: Our growth is not linear but spiral Each turn bringing us closer to ourselves Each cycle healing another generation Each evolution touching past and future Each step forward healing backward and blessing forward

[CLAIMING OUR JOURNEY]

We claim this right Not as those who have arrived But as those who are arriving Like sweet potato vines reaching toward sun Not as those who have apprehended But as those who press toward the mark Not as those who are perfect But as those perfectly committed to growth Not as single points in time But as bridges between generations

[FINAL DECLARATION]

For to truly see into me Is to see the generations that made me Is to see the generations I will influence Is to see the eternal spiral of becoming Is to finally be free

Into Me See Into We See Into Free Into Be Into Grow Into Know Into Flow Through generations below And generations to go

The Invitation: Join the Movement

This manifesto is not just poetry—it's a call to action. It's an invitation to join a movement of Black men committed to emotional liberation and authentic love. This movement includes:

Men who choose therapy over silence. Who see seeking help as strength rather than weakness, who prioritize mental health as much as physical health.

Men who choose vulnerability over invulnerability. Who are willing to share their fears, admit their mistakes, and ask for support when they need it.

Men who choose growth over stagnation. Who see themselves as works in progress, who are committed to continuous learning and development.

Men who choose partnership over dominance. Who see relationships as collaborations rather than competitions, who value their partners' voices and contributions.

Men who choose healing over hurting. Who are committed to breaking cycles of trauma rather than perpetuating them, who choose to heal themselves so they can love others more fully.

Men who choose community over isolation. Who support other men's growth, who create spaces for authentic connection and mutual support.

Men who choose legacy over immediate gratification. Who think about the emotional inheritance they're leaving for their children and communities.

Your Next 30 Days: From Reading to Transformation

Week 1: Assessment and Awareness
- Take the Love Language Assessment in Appendix A
- Share your primary love language with your partner/family
- Identify which love language feels most challenging for you
- Begin one daily practice from your primary chapter

Week 2: Integration and Practice
- Practice expressing love in your partner's primary language daily
- Address any trauma or barriers that limit your love language expression
- Read one additional chapter that focuses on a love language you want to develop
- Schedule time for self-reflection and emotional processing

Week 3: Community and Support
- Find or create a support group focused on emotional growth for Black men
- Share what you've learned with at least one other man who could benefit
- Practice vulnerable communication with someone you trust
- Identify a mentor or therapist who can support your continued growth

Week 4: Legacy and Leadership
- Reflect on the emotional legacy you want to leave for your children
- Begin modeling healthy masculinity for younger men in your community
- Plan for long-term growth and development beyond this 30-day period
- Celebrate the progress you've made and commit to continued transformation

Find Your Tribe

Online Communities:
- Join online forums dedicated to Black male emotional growth and healing
- Connect with other readers of this book through social media groups
- Participate in virtual men's groups focused on emotional intelligence

Local Resources:
- Find culturally competent therapists in your area who understand Black male experiences
- Connect with progressive Black churches that support men's emotional development
- Join or create local men's groups focused on authentic connection and growth

Professional Development:
- Seek out leadership development programs that include emotional intelligence
- Find mentors who model healthy masculinity and emotional maturity
- Consider becoming a mentor to younger Black men who need guidance

The Legacy We're Creating

Every Black man who chooses emotional growth and authentic love is creating a legacy that extends far beyond his individual life. We are:

Healing Generational Trauma: Breaking cycles of emotional suppression, relational dysfunction, and trauma that have been passed down through families for generations.

Redefining Black Masculinity: Creating new models of what it means to be a strong Black man—models that include emotional intelligence, relational skills, and collaborative leadership.

Strengthening Black Families: Building healthier relationships that provide stable, loving foundations for children and communities.

Challenging Systemic Oppression: Refusing to internalize the lies that systems of oppression have told us about our worth, our capacity, and our humanity.

Creating Cultural Change: Shifting the narrative about Black men from deficit-focused to strength-based, from problem-centered to solution-oriented.

Inspiring Future Generations: Showing young Black boys and men that they have choices their fathers and grandfathers didn't have—choices about how to express emotions, build relationships, and define masculinity.

The Promise We Make

As we conclude this journey together, we make this promise—to ourselves, to our families, to our communities, and to future generations:

We promise to continue growing. We will not settle for who we are today but will continue evolving into who we're meant to become.

We promise to love authentically. We will express love in ways that create connection rather than distance, healing rather than harm.

We promise to seek help when we need it. We will not suffer in silence but will reach out for support, guidance, and healing.

We promise to support other men. We will not compete with other men but will collaborate with them in our mutual growth and healing.

We promise to honor our relationships. We will prioritize the people we love and invest in the connections that matter most.

We promise to break harmful cycles. We will not repeat the patterns that hurt us but will create new patterns that heal us.

We promise to model healthy masculinity. We will show the world what strong, emotionally intelligent, relationally skilled Black men look like.

We promise to never give up on love. No matter how many times we've been hurt, disappointed, or rejected, we will continue believing in the power of authentic love to heal and transform.

The Final Word: You Are Enough

As we close this book, remember this truth: You are enough. Not when you get better, not when you heal completely, not when you master all these love languages perfectly. You are enough right now, in this moment, with all your strengths and struggles, all your growth and gaps, all your healing and hurting.

You are enough to be loved. You are enough to love others. You are enough to heal. You are enough to grow. You are enough to change. You are enough to matter.

The world may have told you otherwise. Systems may have suggested you're not enough. People may have treated you as if you're not enough. But they were wrong. You have always been enough, and you will always be enough.

Your journey toward emotional fluency and authentic love is not about becoming enough—it's about recognizing the enough-ness that has always been within you. It's about expressing the love that has always been in your heart. It's about sharing the gifts that have always been part of your soul.

INTO ME SEE: The Invitation to Intimacy

INTO ME SEE. Let people see into you. Let them see your heart, your dreams, your fears, your hopes. Let them see your struggles and your triumphs, your questions and your certainties, your wounds and your healing.

This is the ultimate love language—the courage to be fully seen and the commitment to fully see others. This is intimacy in its truest form—not just physical closeness, but emotional transparency, spiritual connection, and authentic presence.

You have spent too much of your life hiding, protecting, performing, and pretending. You have spent too much energy maintaining masks that keep you safe but also keep you isolated. You have spent too much time being who others wanted you to be instead of who you actually are.

It's time to be seen. It's time to be known. It's time to be loved for who you really are, not who you think you should be.

This is your invitation to intimacy—with yourself, with your partner, with your children, with your community, with your Creator. This is your invitation to love like a man—a whole man, a healed man, a man who knows his worth and shares his heart.

The world needs your authentic self. Your family needs your real heart. Your community needs your genuine voice. Your children need your true example.

Stop hiding. Start healing. Stop performing. Start being. Stop pretending. Start loving.

INTO ME SEE. This is how we love like men—with courage, authenticity, vulnerability, and grace.

This is your declaration. This is your invitation. This is your time.

Love like a man. Love like the man you were created to be.

"The most powerful thing you can do is to be yourself in a world that is constantly trying to make you something else. For Black men, being yourself is not just personal liberation—it's collective revolution." — Michael Darby

Appendix A: Love Language Assessment and Growth Practices

The 7 Love Languages Assessment for Black Men

For each statement below, rate how much it resonates with you on a scale of 1-5: 1 = Doesn't resonate at all 2 = Rarely resonates 3 = Sometimes resonates 4 = Often resonates 5 = Always resonates

Presence as Protection

☐ I show love by being consistently available and reliable ☐ I feel most loved when someone chooses to spend time with me ☐ My presence in difficult situations is how I express care ☐ I demonstrate commitment by showing up, even when it's hard ☐ I feel valued when people appreciate my consistency and availability ☐ I express care by being physically and emotionally present ☐ I feel disconnected when people are too busy to spend time with me ☐ My way of protecting people is by being there with them

Presence as Protection Total: ___/40

Provision as Expression

☐ I express love by taking care of people's needs ☐ I feel valued when people appreciate what I do for them ☐ Working hard for my family is how I show I care ☐ I measure my love by what I'm willing to give or sacrifice ☐ I feel fulfilled when I can provide for others ☐ I show affection by meeting practical needs ☐ I feel unappreciated when my efforts to provide go unnoticed ☐ I believe comprehensive care is the highest form of love

Provision as Expression Total: ___/40

Respect as Intimacy

☐ I need to feel respected before I can be vulnerable ☐ I show love by honoring others' judgment and autonomy ☐ Feeling trusted and valued is essential for my emotional openness ☐ I withdraw when I feel disrespected or criticized ☐ I express care by treating people with dignity and honor ☐ I feel most connected when my competence is acknowledged ☐ I need to know that my decisions and judgment are trusted ☐ I demonstrate love by creating space for others to be themselves

Respect as Intimacy Total: ___/40

Loyalty as Language

☐ I demonstrate love through consistent commitment ☐ Staying power and faithfulness are how I express devotion ☐ I feel most secure in relationships with mutual loyalty ☐ I show care by being dependable and trustworthy ☐ I express affection through long-term commitment ☐ I feel valued when people recognize my faithfulness ☐ I believe loyalty is one of the highest forms of love ☐ I demonstrate care by choosing to stay when things get difficult

Loyalty as Language Total: ___/40

Sacrifice as Devotion

☐ I express love by putting others' needs before my own ☐ Giving up things for people I care about feels natural ☐ I measure love by willingness to sacrifice for each other ☐ Service and selflessness are how I show I care ☐ I feel fulfilled when I can give meaningful gifts of time or resources ☐ I demonstrate affection by going without so others can have ☐ I feel loved when people appreciate my sacrifices ☐ I show care by working hard for the benefit of others

Sacrifice as Devotion Total: ___/40

Affirmation as Healing

☐ I need verbal recognition and appreciation to feel valued ☐ Words of encouragement and praise are essential for my growth ☐ I express love by acknowledging others' character and efforts ☐ Criticism affects me deeply, while affirmation energizes me ☐ I feel connected when people see and name my positive qualities ☐ I demonstrate care by offering specific, meaningful compliments ☐ I need to hear that I'm appreciated and doing things right ☐ I show love by speaking life into people's potential and character

Affirmation as Healing Total: ___/40

Touch as Trust

☐ Physical affection is important for feeling connected ☐ I express care through appropriate physical touch ☐ Non-sexual touch helps me feel safe and loved ☐ Physical closeness is how I both give and receive comfort ☐ I feel valued when people are comfortable being physically affectionate with me ☐ I demonstrate love through hugs, hand-holding, and other appropriate touch ☐ I need physical affection to feel fully loved and accepted ☐ I show care by offering comfort through touch

Touch as Trust Total: ___/40

Interpreting Your Results

Your Primary Love Language: The category with your highest score (usually 25-40 points)

Your Secondary Love Languages: Categories scoring 18-30 points

Growth Areas: Categories scoring below 18 points may represent areas where you can expand your emotional vocabulary

Remember: There are no "wrong" scores. This assessment helps you understand your natural preferences while identifying areas for potential growth.

Daily Growth Practices by Love Language

Presence as Protection - Daily Practices

Morning Practice: Set an intention to be emotionally present, not just physically present, in at least one interaction today.

Midday Check-in: Ask yourself: "Am I here in body only, or am I here with my heart and attention too?"

Evening Reflection: Identify one moment when your presence provided comfort or security for someone else.

Weekly Practice: Have a "presence conversation" with your partner or children about what makes them feel most seen and attended to by you.

Provision as Expression - Daily Practices

Morning Practice: Ask yourself: "What can I provide today beyond money—emotionally, spiritually, or relationally?"

Midday Check-in: Notice opportunities to provide comprehensive care, not just financial support.

Evening Reflection: Acknowledge one way you provided for others today that wasn't financial.

Weekly Practice: Create a "provision plan" that includes all forms of care you want to offer your family.

Respect as Intimacy - Daily Practices

Morning Practice: Set an intention to honor someone's judgment or autonomy in a specific way today.

Midday Check-in: Notice when you feel respected or disrespected, and how that affects your emotional availability.

Evening Reflection: Identify one way you showed respect for someone's dignity today.

Weekly Practice: Have a conversation with your partner about what respect looks like in your relationship.

Loyalty as Language - Daily Practices

Morning Practice: Identify one specific way you can demonstrate commitment and faithfulness today.

Midday Check-in: Ask yourself: "Am I being actively loyal or passively loyal in my relationships?"

Evening Reflection: Recognize one moment when you chose commitment over convenience.

Weekly Practice: Communicate your loyalty to someone important to you, explaining what your commitment means.

Sacrifice as Devotion - Daily Practices

Morning Practice: Choose one meaningful sacrifice to make today, but ensure it comes from abundance, not depletion.

Midday Check-in: Ask yourself: "Am I sacrificing from love or from guilt/obligation?"

Evening Reflection: Assess whether your giving today was sustainable and healthy.

Weekly Practice: Evaluate the balance between giving and receiving in your most important relationships.

Affirmation as Healing - Daily Practices

Morning Practice: Identify one person who could benefit from specific, genuine affirmation today.

Midday Check-in: Notice negative self-talk and counter it with affirming truth about yourself.

Evening Reflection: Acknowledge one way you were affirmed today, or one way you affirmed someone else.

Weekly Practice: Keep a record of meaningful affirmations you receive to review during difficult times.

Touch as Trust - Daily Practices

Morning Practice: Set an intention to offer appropriate physical comfort or affection to someone today.

Midday Check-in: Notice your comfort level with physical affection and what might increase that comfort.

Evening Reflection: Identify one moment when touch (given or received) communicated care or connection.

Weekly Practice: Communicate with your partner about physical affection preferences and boundaries.

Appendix B: Resources for Continued Healing

Books for Continued Growth

Emotional Intelligence and Relationships

- "Emotional Intelligence 2.0" by Travis Bradberry and Jean Greaves
- "The Emotionally Intelligent Man" by Karla McLaren
- "Getting the Love You Want" by Harville Hendrix
- "Hold Me Tight" by Sue Johnson
- "The Seven Principles for Making Marriage Work" by John Gottman

Black Male Psychology and Healing

- "Post Traumatic Slave Syndrome" by Joy DeGruy
- "My Grandmother's Hands" by Resmaa Menakem
- "The Miseducation of the Negro" by Carter G. Woodson

- "We Real Cool" by bell hooks
- "Homecoming" by Thema Bryant

Trauma and Healing

- "The Body Keeps the Score" by Bessel van der Kolk
- "It Didn't Start With You" by Mark Wolynn
- "Waking the Tiger" by Peter Levine
- "Complex PTSD" by Pete Walker

Masculinity and Identity

- "King, Warrior, Magician, Lover" by Robert Moore and Douglas Gillette
- "Deep Secrets" by Niobe Way
- "The Way of the Superior Man" by David Deida
- "Iron John" by Robert Bly

Therapy and Professional Support

Finding Culturally Competent Therapists

Psychology Today: Use their therapist finder with filters for race/ethnicity and specialties

- Website: psychologytoday.com

- Filter for African American therapists

- Look for specialties in trauma, relationships, and men's issues

Therapy for Black Girls: Also has resources for Black men
- Website: therapyforblackgirls.com

- National directory of Black mental health professionals

National Alliance on Mental Illness (NAMI): Local chapters with resources
- Website: nami.org

- Culturally competent treatment resources

Black Mental Health Alliance: Professional directory and resources
- Website: blackmentalhealth.com

Types of Therapy That May Be Helpful

Individual Therapy:
- Cognitive Behavioral Therapy (CBT)

- Emotionally Focused Therapy (EFT)

- Eye Movement Desensitization and Reprocessing (EMDR) for trauma

- Acceptance and Commitment Therapy (ACT)

Couples Therapy:
- Emotionally Focused Couples Therapy

- Gottman Method Couples Therapy

- Imago Relationship Therapy

Group Therapy:
- Men's therapy groups
- Trauma recovery groups
- Relationship skills groups
- Black men's support groups

Online Resources and Communities

Websites and Blogs

- **Therapy for Black Men**: therapyforblackmen.com
- **Black Male Development**: blackmaledevelopment.org
- **National Alliance on Mental Illness**: nami.org
- **Crisis Text Line**: Text HOME to 741741

Podcasts for Black Male Growth

- "Therapy for Black Girls" (also addresses men's issues)
- "The Black Male Perspective"
- "Conversations with Black Men"
- "Masculine Psychology" by David Tian
- "The School of Greatness" by Lewis Howes

Apps for Mental Health and Mindfulness

- **Headspace**: Meditation and mindfulness

- **Calm**: Sleep stories, meditation, relaxation

- **BetterHelp**: Online therapy platform

- **Talkspace**: Text-based therapy

- **Sanvello**: Anxiety and mood tracking

Community Resources

Men's Groups and Organizations

National Organizations:
- **National Association of Social Workers**: Men's groups directory

- **ManKind Project**: Men's personal development

- **Promise Keepers**: Faith-based men's organization

- **100 Black Men**: Mentorship and community service

Local Resources to Seek:
- Church-based men's ministries

- Community center men's groups

- Barbershop talk groups

- Father support groups

- Professional men's associations

Crisis Resources

National Suicide Prevention Lifeline: 988 **Crisis Text Line:** Text HOME to 741741 **National Domestic Violence Hotline**: 1-800-799-7233 **SAMHSA National Helpline**: 1-800-662-4357

Educational and Professional Development

Leadership and Professional Growth

- **Executive coaching** with focus on emotional intelligence
- **Leadership development programs** that include relationship skills
- **Professional mentorship** from emotionally mature leaders
- **Continuing education** in communication and conflict resolution

Parenting Resources

- "The 5 Love Languages of Children" by Gary Chapman
- "Raising Black Boys" by Jawanza Kunjufu
- "Strong Fathers, Strong Daughters" by Meg Meeker
- Local parenting classes and support groups

Appendix C: Quick Reference Guide

Daily Love Language Check-In

Morning Question: "How can I express my primary love language today in a refined way?"

Midday Question: "Am I expressing love from fullness or depletion? From healing or hurt?"

Evening Question: "How did my partner/family express love in their language today? How can I acknowledge it?"

Weekly Question: "What growth am I seeing in our love language fluency? What still needs work?"

Love Language Emergency Kit

When Your Partner Feels Unloved:

1. **Stop and Ask**: "What would help you feel most loved right now?"

2. **Listen Without Defending**: Hear their heart, not just their words

3. **Acknowledge**: "I can see that you need ___ ___ from me"

4. **Act**: Do something in their love language within 24 hours

5. **Follow Up**: "How did that feel? What else can I do?"

When You Feel Disrespected or Criticized:

1. **Pause**: Take 3 deep breaths before responding

2. **Name It**: "I'm feeling disrespected right now"

3. **Seek Understanding**: "Help me understand your heart behind what you just said"

4. **Express Your Need**: "I need to feel respected in order to be vulnerable with you"

5. **Collaborate**: "How can we handle this differently next time?"

When Communication Breaks Down:

1. **Call a Timeout**: "Let's take a 20-minute break and come back"

2. **Get Curious**: "What love language is trying to be expressed here?"

3. **Translate**: "It sounds like you need _____, and I need _____"

4. **Find Common Ground**: "We both want to feel loved and respected"

5. **Try Again**: "Let's try this conversation again with fresh hearts"

The Love Language Fluency Scale

Level 1: Awareness (0-3 months)

- You can identify your primary love language
- You recognize when others express love differently than you do
- You're learning about the other 6 love languages

Level 2: Basic Fluency (3-12 months)

- You can express love in 2-3 different love languages
- You're healing from trauma that limits your expression
- You're practicing daily growth exercises

Level 3: Intermediate Fluency (1-2 years)

- You can communicate in 4-5 love languages comfortably
- You can translate between different love languages in relationships
- You're helping others understand love language differences

Level 4: Advanced Fluency (2+ years)

- You're comfortable expressing and receiving love in all 7 languages

- You can teach and mentor others in love language development
- You're creating love language-rich environments in your family and community

Level 5: Master Level (5+ years)

- Love language fluency has become natural and unconscious
- You're breaking generational cycles and creating new patterns
- You're leading cultural change in how Black men express emotion and love

Common Love Language Mistakes to Avoid

For Men:

- **Assuming your love language is everyone's love language**
- **Using love languages to avoid accountability** ("This is just how I show love")
- **Neglecting your own healing work** while trying to love others
- **Becoming rigid about "your" love language** instead of remaining flexible
- **Using love languages to manipulate or control** others

For Partners:

- **Dismissing his love language** as invalid or insufficient

- **Expecting immediate change** instead of supporting gradual growth

- **Making it about you** instead of understanding his journey

- **Comparing him to other men** instead of celebrating his unique expression

- **Using love languages as weapons** during conflict

Conversation Starters for Deeper Connection

For Romantic Relationships:

- "What made you feel most loved as a child?"

- "How do you know when I'm really listening to you?"

- "What's one way I could show love that would surprise you?"

- "How has your way of expressing love changed as you've grown?"

- "What do you need from me when you're struggling or stressed?"

For Father-Child Relationships:

- "What's your favorite way for us to spend time together?"

- "How do you like to be encouraged when you're trying hard at something?"

- "What makes you feel most proud of yourself?"

- "How can I support you better when you're having a difficult day?"

- "What do you want to remember most about our relationship?"

For Friendships and Brotherhood:

- "What does loyalty mean to you in friendship?"

- "How do you prefer to be supported when you're going through something?"

- "What's the most meaningful way someone has shown they care about you?"

- "How can we create more authentic connection in our friendship?"

- "What do you need from me to feel comfortable being vulnerable?"

Your Personal Love Language Action Plan

Next 30 Days:

☐ Complete the Love Language Assessment ☐ Share results with your most important relationships ☐ Choose one love language to focus on developing ☐ Begin daily practices from that chapter ☐ Address any trauma that limits your expression

Next 90 Days:

☐ Expand to practicing 2-3 love languages regularly ☐ Have love language conversations with family members ☐ Seek therapy or counseling if needed for deeper healing ☐ Join or create a men's group focused on emotional growth ☐ Start mentoring or supporting another man's growth

Next Year:

☐ Develop fluency in 4-5 love languages ☐ Create love language-rich environment in your home ☐ Teach love language concepts to others ☐ Continue healing work and personal development ☐ Measure the impact on your relationships and family

Long-term (2-5 years):

☐ Master all 7 love languages in your personal relationships ☐ Lead cultural change in your community ☐ Break generational cycles for your children ☐ Mentor other Black men in emotional development ☐ Create lasting legacy of healthy masculinity

About the author

Michael Darby is a Black man, father, and passionate advocate for Black male emotional liberation. He holds a degree in Communications and has spent years in his own healing journey—doing the hard work of therapy, self-reflection, and growth that this book calls other men to embrace.

This book was born not from academic study alone, but from lived experience. Michael is simply an everyday Black man who chose to work on himself, who refused to accept the limitations placed on Black male emotional expression, and who believes that Black men deserve the right to define what love looks like for us.

Through his own therapy journey, countless conversations with other Black men, extensive research, and deep commitment to breaking generational cycles, Michael has gathered the insights and frameworks shared in these pages. He has learned from therapists, read extensively, engaged with research, and most importantly—listened to the hearts and stories of Black men who, like him, are choosing growth over stagnation, healing over hurt.

Michael is not a licensed therapist or counselor. He is a Black man who has done the work and is committed to helping other good Black men understand that we have the right to determine what love needs to look, be, and sound like for us. His authority comes not from degrees on a wall, but from scars turned to wisdom, pain transformed into purpose, and the courage to vulnerability that he asks of every reader.

This is his first book, written for every Black man who has been told he doesn't know how to love when the truth is we've been loving in languages the world wouldn't learn to speak. Michael lives with his three children, who continue to teach him about the courage required for genuine intimacy and the power of unconditional love.

For more resources and to connect with Michael's ongoing work, visit: www.7lovelanguagesofblackmen.com

"The most revolutionary thing a Black man can do is heal himself, love authentically, and teach other men to do the same. This is how we change the world—one heart, one relationship, one generation at a time."
— Michael Darby

www.ingramcontent.com/pod-product-compliance
Lightning Source LLC
Chambersburg PA
CBHW052130030426
42337CB00028B/5101